Expansion

Expansion
How Natural Gas Fuels are Reshaping Transportation in America

By Bryan Luftglass

Expansion
How Natural Gas Fuels are Reshaping
Transportation in America

© 2014 Bryan Luftglass

Published by:
Bryan Luftglass
12082 Big Cottonwood Canyon
Solitude, Utah 84121

ISBN 978-1-4951-2491-4

Typeset by Allzone Digital Services Limited
Printed in the United States of America

CONTENTS

ACKNOWLEDGEMENTS

During the past decade, I've met some of the pioneers, early adopters, change agents and torch carriers in the natural gas vehicle fuels business. It is to those individuals, some of whom are profiled here, I dedicate this book. I further want to acknowledge those same who so generously contributed their time, support, important facts, anecdotes, opinions, rants and criticisms to help prepare this material.

Thanks must also go to Nick Garafola, Frank Chapel at Apache and Pat LaStrapes who generously contributed their insights and precious time to perform deep edits of the book. I also appreciate the "light" editors, my friends who also gave me great feedback, like Roger Neville, Phil Smith and my daughter Kim.

Finally, while I tried my best to acknowledge all of the major champions of the natural gas fuels industry – people who have combined passion, intelligence, commitment, savvy and sometimes stubbornness to develop it to the point we are at today and will be tomorrow – my deepest apologies go in advance to those I have inadvertently overlooked.

FOREWORD

The emergence of the natural gas fuels marketplace has not been without fits and starts. Nevertheless, the fundamentals have inevitably led us to this juncture, as we ponder not whether – but rather when – the market will bolt upward and into the steep slope of the adoption curve.

Veteran insider Bryan Luftglass, in this concise, pithy history, brings keen insights into the underpinnings of the nascent natural gas fuels market, a natural bedfellow of the shale boom. Written in a refreshing anecdotal style, with chapter headings celebrating our pop-rock history, *Expansion* is a can't-put-down read for those active in this space and others interested in fuels, transportation and business in general. Importantly, the story is just beginning to unfold and I fully expect that this seminal work of depth and substance will lead to future editions and new books as we catalog developments and attempt to understand, quantify and predict the path of this market as it develops.

Serving as vice chairman of the third and fourth World LNG Fuels Conferences (held in 2013 and 2014) and as a consultant to the industry, I have been fortunate enough to develop my own independent knowledge of the individuals, companies, events, outcomes, experiments, deals, failures and successes mentioned. Suffice it to say that, from the standpoints of materiality and relevance, Bryan has, in my opinion, included everything of consequence vital to a well-rounded, fair, first-time-ever account of the industry.

Looking beyond the scope of this book, I believe we must consider the field of new entrants into the North American natural gas fuels market. Deep-pocketed Asian investors have been developing the same market at home and eyeing the space in this country. Some are already making moves to invest and establish positions through strategic partnerships. That comment extends to investment in shale gas production as well. My colleagues at Enovation Partners are already helping a few of these giants.

In the marketplace both here and abroad, we continue to set new milestones. To take but one example, the LNG-fueled luxury ferry, the Francisco, is the world's fastest ship, clocking 58.1 knots and capable of transporting 1,000 passengers and 150 cars between Buenos Aires and Montevideo. We must continue to keep a wide eye open to developments in South America, Europe and Asia and be prepared to adapt and adopt the best ideas here.

Technology is synchronizing with the needs of the marketplace. Natural gas compression and liquefaction developments will accelerate in the next few years. Engine and fuel storage technology continues to push forward, and research organizations like the Gas Technology Institute, working with the industry, will help in generating new ideas, breakthroughs, better economics and better performance as the natural gas fuels space continues to evolve.

Pat LaStrapes

PREFACE

Change doesn't happen merely by accident, destiny or fate. Change happens through a chaotic combination of individual determination, effort and plans as well as by accident. The backdrop for the natural gas fuels industry involves engines, vehicles and fuel sources, which themselves have undergone such metamorphoses.

Engines for power have been theorized for over two thousand years and built for practical use since at least the early 1600s. Some two hundred years ago, Robert Fulton overcame tremendous odds to turn his derided "Folly" into a steam engine-driven steamboat capable of transporting goods and people much more efficiently than anyone (save, perhaps a Leonardo daVinci) could have dreamed of earlier.

Fifty years later, determined businessmen and engineers pushed, stumbled and eventually persevered to capture large amounts of underground oil, forming the backdrop for a revolution in fuels for transportation and heating. In a whirl of technical marvels, inventors like Herbert Akroyd-Stuart and Rudolf Diesel were able to harness the ability of oil to explode under pressure to create the internal combustion engine, while Jean J. Lenoir, Nikolaus Otto and others learned how to combine sparking with highly-flammable hydrocarbons like gasoline to create the gasoline powered engine. Then, within another fifty years, Henry Ford, Ransom Olds, Karl Benz and others developed means to efficiently build, distribute, sell and service trucks and automobiles using these engines.

The process that got us to that point was not straightforward. Change was often sparked by an apple-falling-on-Newton's-head-to-discover-gravity sort of "Aha" moment.

Once an idea took shape, it then took bold, determined individuals to create new companies or to work within existing corporations, governments and institutions to carry those concepts forward. In some cases, those ideas became products that became successes.

†††

Before delving further into the subject of natural gas fuels, I wish to share my own relevant journey of discovery.

I was trained academically in the physical and natural sciences including geology, biology, chemistry, physics, oceanography, climatology and other areas that don't fit neatly into any one of these categories, then spent much of my career as a consultant applying that knowledge to a diverse set of business topics.

Sometimes my work took me into the world of transportation fuels and vehicles. Clients would ask questions like: What's the price of oil going to be in a year (or five or ten years)? How will that affect gasoline and diesel prices? Could such and such alternative fuel (say, biodiesel, methanol or hydrogen) become significant and how could I develop a business around that outlook?

Along the way, I was of course exposed to natural gas fuels. And I distinctly remember thinking "Yes, compressed natural gas could make sense. But, the other approach – cooling it down hundreds of degrees until gaseous natural gas becomes liquefied natural gas and then heating it back up to combust it – that makes no sense at all." So, I was surprised when my career brought me into a large, global company that was looking for areas of growth and I stumbled, serendipitously or accidentally (you may choose which) into this liquefied natural gas thing. I was able to help lead them into that field and worked in the business for much of a ten year stretch. (Frankly, ten years is well past my usual attention span). During that time, I realized I was wrong: LNG can, in fact, be a viable fuel and will sit alongside CNG as a product of significant importance.

I now hope that my background and immersion in the natural gas fuels industry can be of value to you in helping to understand how this industry will help satisfy our future transportation needs.

†††

Looking at the history of the natural gas fueling industry, you can make out the curves and hills on the road that stretched from early concepts to survive the challenges from other ideas, pursuits and happenstance to make it to some significant level of success and sustainability. But, there were plenty of dead ends. There were also apparent dead ends where, lo and behold, something changed allowing the progress to continue again – like a street in some California housing development that ends in a cul-de-sac until it's later broken through so new homes can be built along the now-extended roadway.

So, here we stand. There are roughly a billion cars and trucks operating around the world that were built to run on gasoline and diesel fuel, not natural gas fuels. But that's beginning to change. And about to change a lot more.

†††

I should explain what this book is not before sharing what it is. It is not a treatise on why America should use natural gas-fueled cars and trucks, although the "why" can't be entirely separated out from the rest of the story. I also don't offer a concrete set of predictions of how this revolution will end. However, there are ideas I'm happy to share that provide clues on the possible direction and I do provide a section on what's likely next and what could be. Some of the current business concepts will surely bear the scars of obsolescence like those endured by any new industry.

This book is also not a comprehensive history of natural gas vehicles and fuels. It does, however, tell a story, providing a portal into the history of the ideas that have enabled the industry to get to this point. It also identifies some keenly important people that received the spark of inspiration or experienced the unintended consequences of happy accidents to help propel the industry and further identifies some of the companies that have carried the torch, all to get us to this point.

The book is organized into four parts. In the first, we'll trace the history of natural gas fuels from the early 1990s (when it appeared that natural gas vehicles would take off, spurred by government policy) until around 2007 when the business was inching along at not much more than a snail's pace. The second part focuses on the past half-dozen years, when there have been dramatic advancements in technology and interest that, combined with a truly massive shift in natural gas production technology, have taken us to a growth inflection point.

The third section puts a stake of currency in the ground, identifying where we are now and how this will propel us into the future. In the final few chapters, we'll take out the crystal ball, hazy as it inevitably is, and see where the natural gas fuels revolution can take us.

The story already has a long history, but most of the history has yet to take place.

INTRODUCTION "Science and Faith"
(The Script)

A round the world and off the radar screens of most Americans, people in many countries have been converting their taxis, personal cars, buses and other vehicles to run on natural gas for about a century.

Natural gas, – also called methane – is a gas under normal earthly conditions, so it's hard to pump, pipe, store in a fuel tank or use. In comparison, as liquids, gasoline and diesel are easy to pump, pipe, store and use, so they are far more popular vehicle fuels. These beneficial properties have enabled the widespread use of those petroleum products as fuels and driven up their value.

Even adding in the cost to modify the natural gas so it's a storable, usable fuel, it's still far cheaper than gasoline and diesel. So, millions of people motivated to save money and willing to tinker with their cars and other vehicles have switched in large numbers in dozens of countries. Comparatively speaking, the U.S. has been slow to adopt the use of natural gas fuels. As one minister of energy for a resource-rich, but otherwise less developed, country once told me "We're happy to sell expensive oil to you in America and keep our cheap natural gas for use at home."

Not that we've been completely silent on the subject in the U.S. In fact, there were natural gas cars built in the U.S. at the same time that gasoline, diesel, steam, and electricity vied for early dominance in the twilight of the horse-drawn buggy era. But interest in natural gas fuels didn't take off until just a few years ago, before which we were flat-lining at a hundred thousand vehicles, give or take, for several decades. Maybe that's why methane is pronounced "meh-thane" in the U.S. ("meh" as in it doesn't really matter) while it's pronounced "me (as in me, myself and I) thane" in much of the rest of the world. It's only been in the past few years that we've leapt up closer to two hundred thousand natural gas vehicles in the U.S. and demand is now accelerating.

Modifying natural gas into a usable fuel is quite straight-forward. Simply, compressed natural gas or "CNG" is merely natural gas taken from a pipeline and squeezed into a higher-pressure form. Pipelines are already carrying natural gas in a 'mildly' compressed form, meaning a few pounds per square inch (psi) up to a few hundred psi. However, to store enough natural gas in a car or truck for practical use, you need to compress it up to at least 3,000 to 3,600 psi, which is 200–250 times the pressure found at sea level.

Instead of compressing methane, you can cool it down to a dramatically cold minus 260° Fahrenheit. This is cold enough to create liquefied natural gas (LNG) in much the same way steam changes into water when it is cooled below 212° Fahrenheit. In liquefied form, the natural gas is 600 times as dense as gaseous natural gas (again, referenced to sea level pressure) and you can pump, pipe, store and use it nearly as easily as diesel or gasoline fuel.

If you're in the market for a new car or truck, you can buy a natural gas-fueled vehicle right now. Or, you can find a qualified company that will convert your existing car or truck so you can run it on natural gas. Then, you can pump the gas into your fuel tank from a dispenser pretty much the same way you would pump gasoline. If you live anywhere near a major city or close to an interstate highway, you'll probably be able to find CNG stations where you can refuel for at least $1.00 per gallon less than the gasoline dispenser a few feet away.

It's very possible the truck picking up your garbage or the intra-city bus you ride or airport shuttle taking you to your flight are running on natural gas. UPS may be transporting your packages in heavy-duty trucks that also run on natural gas. In a few years, the cruise ship you'll be taking to the

Caribbean could very well also run on natural gas. In short, natural gas fueling is quietly revolutionizing how we travel and how goods are shipped, with the promise that money will be saved, air quality will improve and oil spills will be avoided, all the while displacing imported foreign oil.

This rolling thunder of change is not entirely unexpected. For decades, forecasters have been predicting a gradual shift from other fuels to natural gas. In fact, for many years, Shell (Oil!) used a chart to describe how the world, over hundreds and hundreds of years, shifted from wood as the primary energy source, to coal and then oil. Their forecast has shown us now on the cusp of a further transformation to natural gas, and ultimately and eventually to hydrogen.

Several threads run through this long-term scenario. First, the change from wood to coal to oil and now natural gas can be explained by improving infrastructure to get the fuel to where it's needed – wood could be gathered virtually anywhere and hauled in a cart or on one's back, coal could be hauled in a cart and later by truck, and oil by truck, rail and pipelines. Natural gas pretty much has to go by pipeline, although a little bit gets moved by ships and trucks.

The fact is that 2.4 million miles of natural gas pipelines span the U.S. We're heavily reliant on natural gas to heat our homes and produce power, so much so that natural gas already accounts for one-quarter of America's total energy consumption. We just haven't yet taken advantage of this infrastructure much to fuel our vehicles.

Another inherent aspect of this long-term trend is that we're experiencing an evolution to cleaner fuels, which benefits both the environment and human health. Cleanliness can be measured in many ways, and one relatively technical explanation is drawn from the fact these are all (save hydrogen) hydrocarbons, that is to say they are made predominantly from hydrogen and carbon. The amount of (dirty burning) carbon to (clean burning) hydrogen decreases from wood to coal to oil to natural gas. Finally, with hydrogen, we jettison the carbon entirely from the product.

When burned as a vehicle fuel, natural gas is inherently cleaner than gasoline and, even more so, diesel. Less soot is generated, which is clearly beneficial to lung and heart health, and provides an improvement to visibility, which is especially valued in and around our national parks. Also, lower amounts of smog-producing emissions are generated. This can be offset to a point: diesel engines can be brought to relative environmental parity with natural gas by adding filters, catalysts and chemicals that condition the tailpipe emissions.

Of course, gasoline and diesel use won't disappear (for quite awhile, at least!) and other alternatives like plug-in electrics, propane and fuel-cell propelled hydrogen vehicles exist. But, natural gas will be an important fuel – a fuel of choice and possibly *the* fuel of choice. There are already signs of this, like the fact that one-half of all the new home trash collection trucks being bought in the U.S. today are fueled by natural gas and roughly one out of five of all transit buses in operation are running on it too.

†††

That there's a natural gas fuel revolution underway in the American transportation system is obvious only to those people who have been keeping a close watch on it from inside the industry. It's been slowly and quietly gaining speed and momentum, but only reached a tipping point in the past few years. This revolution allows most anyone running a car or light-duty truck, as well as companies operating large truck fleets, ships or railroads to both save money and to lessen impacts on the environment. This natural gas fuels revolution doesn't save consumers money at the expense of the environment or improve the environment at a premium cost. Nor is there a penalty in performance, like sluggish acceleration. Such a combination of benefits with no major downside is highly unusual.

The quietness of this revolution is not for lack of trying by the revolution's leaders. They just haven't captured the popular imagination of, say, plug-in electric vehicles that are exemplified by the Chevy Volt, Teslas and a few other cars, or of hydrogen fuel cell vehicles.

Some of these natural gas fuel leaders, including entrepreneurs, pioneering engineers, out-of-the box thinkers and jumpers-on-the bandwagon have been toiling for ten, twenty and, in many cases, even more years trying to overcome the obstacles needed to bring natural gas fuels into the mainstream. Most of them were determined to build the business bottom-up, getting cars, buses and trucks running natural gas fuels on our highways and in our cities.

Then, from left field (actually, fields where gas & oil are produced) came successful trials of natural gas fuels in non-vehicle applications where huge engines – over 2,000 horsepower each – have traditionally burned a lot of diesel fuel. Those successes have opened the door to natural gas fuels being used more and more in other "high horsepower" engines like those in ships and boats, railroad locomotives and oil & gas "hydraulic fracturing" equipment. Then, just to bring things full circle, *those* successes have now further opened the door to meaningful momentum in cars, buses and trucks.

†††

Where are we now and where could we go? Even now, if you take a shuttle bus or taxi at Los Angeles International, Dallas Fort Worth, both major airports in Chicago, Seattle-Tacoma or many other airports in the U.S., chances are you're in a vehicle that uses natural gas fuels. Within the past few years, it's a pretty safe bet that if you've seen tractor trailers run by such mega-corporations as UPS, Frito-Lay, Proctor & Gamble, Swift Transportation, Central Freight Lines and Ryder, at least some of them were running on natural gas fuels. If the trash trucks picking up the garbage from your home or apartment building are suspiciously quiet, they're running on natural gas fuels.

If you take a cruise around or after the year 2020 from the Pacific Northwest up to Alaska or from Florida to the Caribbean, there's more than a decent chance it'll be running on natural gas fuels. Even that freight train you pass by may be fueled with it in a few years. If your home is served by natural gas, like half the homes in the U.S. are, within a few years you'll be able to install an inexpensive appliance in your garage that will let you refuel your family car with natural gas, saving a substantial amount over the cost of gasoline.

As suggested above, the U.S. isn't alone in moving to natural gas fuels and vehicles; it's just behind most of the rest of the world. Globally, there are 20 million vehicles that run on compressed or liquefied natural gas. While there are only somewhere between one hundred and two hundred thousand natural gas vehicles (NGVs) in the U.S., such diverse countries as Brazil, Argentina, China, India, Iran and Pakistan each have over one million NGVs and Italy has over seven hundred fifty thousand. Our country accounts for twenty percent of all vehicles worldwide and, at best, only one percent of all NGVs.

Low natural gas prices, whether due to local abundance or government policies, have enabled such large numbers of NGVs in other countries. Now that the U.S. and Canada are experiencing massive development of unconventional natural gas resources – spurred by the adoption of new technologies – we also have an abundant supply of natural gas at low prices. As a direct result, we will see rapidly growing levels of natural gas vehicles in North America.

The story already has a long history, but most of the history has yet to take place.

PART I: 1992–2007

1

"Sowing Seeds"
(Jesus and Mary Chain)

T he seeds of this revolution were planted over twenty years ago and sprouted in rather unpredictable ways, much like a tree that needs to adapt to the fertility of its soil, bend with the wind and grow in the direction of the sun. The seeds were planted with the hope, and even some expectation, that they would sprout and grow quickly. It didn't quite work out that way; the tree has grown slowly, fittingly, sometimes seeing its branches pared back or even broken. But it is now starting to bloom beyond the stage where its sustainability is in question and we are just starting to reap the benefits of its fruit.

The history of natural gas-fueled cars goes way, way back and it's possible to trace activity and excitement in them well before the 1990s. For instance, just as LNG plants were being built to serve gas utility needs in the 1960s, so too did utilities have a small presence building CNG fueling stations to serve light-duty vehicles. Even back then, it was possible to pick up a trade journal and read about natural gas-fueled vehicles having reached a turning point. In 1970 the Bonneville Flats speed record of 622 miles per hour was set by the 'Blue Flame', which was equipped to burn LNG.

Many early natural gas-fueled vehicle inventors, mechanics and garage tinkerers from that era are still around. But the modern era of natural gas fueling can be traced to the early 1990s when the Federal government got more involved.

Buried in the provisions of the U.S. Energy Policy Act of 1992 (EPACT for short) and behind the much more sensational mandate that required low-flush toilets, were requirements addressing our heavy reliance on imported oil used to make gasoline. As part of EPACT, government agencies were told to invest a large share of their new vehicle purchases in cars and trucks capable of running on alternative fuels. The logic was that forcing purchases of alternative fuel vehicles would encourage the private sector to build fueling stations, which would then enable more people to buy alternative fuel vehicles, fostering yet more fueling stations, and so forth.

Having all of these stations was intended to eventually make it more palatable for any old Joe or Jane to buy an alternative fuel sedan or family station wagon. The push by the Federal government was well-intentioned, but in the end didn't have legs.

In the case of natural gas, most of the subject fleet managers bought multi-fuel-capable cars – vans and trucks able to run on both gasoline and natural gas. These vehicles had separate tanks to store both and just required a flip of a switch to go from one fuel to the other.*

Sure enough, close to one thousand compressed natural gas stations were built around the U.S. For many of these, companies adept at building compressors or packaging compressors with the other equipment needed to build complete stations sold this equipment to project developers. Many of the compressor and station builders operating then continue in business to this day. To point out a few names with a long history, the Ariel Corporation has been a leading family-owned manufacturer of compressors, including for CNG stations, while a distributor of theirs, ANGI Energy Systems, has remained a large builder of CNG stations.** Similarly, companies like Tulsa Gas Technologies and Kraus Global, to name a few

---

* The simplicity of this approach was possible because natural gas burns in a typical car's "spark-ignited" engine like gasoline does.
** It was announced in mid-2014 that the fuel dispenser company Gilbarco Veeder-Root would acquire ANGI, a move that is indicative of the mainstreaming of the natural gas fuels industry today.

others, have a long history manufacturing and selling the dispensers used to build CNG stations.

Many of the CNG station developers were local gas utilities who also converted their own fleet cars, vans and service trucks to natural gas. The whole program, well-intentioned as it was, fell apart. First, a thousand stations was not enough to allow for widespread adoption of natural gas.* Consumers often had to go significantly out of their way to refuel or had to plan their trips around the ability to find a refueling station on their way. On top of that, the cars only had natural gas tanks that held the equivalent of a handful of gasoline gallons, so if you wanted to use the natural gas, you had to refuel the cars a lot. Like "every day" a lot.

The way the stations were operated also didn't always help matters. A CNG station's job is to pressurize the methane up to something like 250 times normal sea-level pressure and store it under high pressure in large cylinders. This job required some rather complex equipment and, without enough maintenance personnel at the time, it wasn't long before vehicle owners with nearly empty fuel tanks often encountered non-functioning stations, thus becoming disillusioned with the experiment. The limitations of the fueling stations tarnished the idea of relying on natural gas as an everyday transportation fuel.

The stations' compressors and storage tanks installed at that time were often not designed for heavy-duty public use and thus could not keep up with the vehicle filling speed consumers demand. This meant that "Joe" could drive in and then fill his car with three or four gallons of fuel in 5 minutes, but Jane following right behind might need 10 minutes, while the next poor soul might be standing there for 20 minutes for his or her few gallons. This limitation tried the patience of the earliest adopters further, to the point where the savings just didn't make up for the hassle. Even the drivers of vehicles

---

* In comparison, there were over two hundred thousand gasoline stations at the time.

owned by the utilities that built the stations for the most part opted to refill with gasoline, not "gas".

One of the utilities that invested in CNG stations was Southern California Gas, which built a network of stations in the late 1980s and early 1990s. They eventually ran afoul of critics who believed that local utilities had an unfair advantage in the transportation fuel market and so should not be allowed to build, own or operate CNG stations. (The battle over the desirability of utilities operating in CNG rages to this day in some places.) A lawsuit was filed requiring Southern California Gas to divest these stations and a new company emerged simultaneously that was able to secure them in 1997 for practically cents on the dollar.

The company that bought these stations was founded by T. Boone Pickens, a long-time oil magnate, as well as a 1980s takeover artist (and sometimes referred to as a greenmailer). Pickens predicted in 1997 that oil would top $100 per barrel, thus virtually assuring the future of natural gas fuels. However, timing can be everything in business and soon after his new Pickens Fuels Corporation took over the California stations, oil prices fell to $10 per barrel. This resulted in gasoline and diesel prices of close to $1.00 per gallon, which was not much above the price for natural gas fuels. There was simply not enough of a savings to justify investment in natural gas vehicles without significant government incentives.

In spite of the poor economic conditions for investment, Pickens continued to believe in the economic potential of natural gas as a transportation fuel and repeated the same approach he had taken with Southern California Gas. He purchased other companies that owned CNG station networks, such as Blue Energy based in Colorado. Pickens also bought a British Columbia fueling company, BCG Fuels, as well as other existing stations (as before, often at great savings).

By the time Pickens Fuels and BCG were incorporated and renamed as Clean Energy Fuels in 2001, the company was so successful vacuuming up other CNG suppliers that companies were started up specifically with plans to invest, grow and then exit the business by selling out to Clean Energy. (As savvy as Clean Energy was, they appear to have been able to avoid buying start-ups that were over-priced.)

Another natural gas fuels company was started in 1991 by Cy Wagner and Jack Brown, who ran the oil and gas producing company Wagner & Brown LLC from Midland, TX. These men ran in the same circles as Boone Pickens and entering the business – by acquiring a company called Pinnacle CNG Systems – could have been considered a "keeping up with the Joneses" move. Pinnacle's main claim was ownership of a unique compressor called the hydraulic intensifier, which allowed vehicle tanks to get filled at the highest rates possible without expending huge amounts of energy. Wagner & Brown leveraged this technology to subsequently package, build and own or operate 20 CNG stations.

Pinnacle provided Wagner & Brown with more of a hobby than an outright attack on the market until they bought another CNG company named Trillium CNG that was focused on building large refueling stations. With Trillium, they could compete with Clean Energy Fuels in the bus transit space, which was the hottest market for CNG at the time. In pursuing the bus business, Trillium focused on building new transit stations, while Boone often took a more acquisitive approach, buying discounted existing assets.

At about the same time Pickens and Wagner and Brown began to focus on acquiring these CNG stations, another individual named Ken Kelley launched the modern-era commercial liquefied natural gas – LNG – fuels industry.*

---

* As we'll see later, Pickens' company has since become the market leader in LNG fuels and Ken Kelley is now developing CNG-related technologies.

2

"Father and Son"

(Cat Stevens)

In parallel with the CNG industry, the supply and use of LNG for transportation also began to grow. The 1990s were a seminal decade for LNG, including the construction of the first commercial LNG fueling station in 1991 by the still-current industry leader Chart Industries and the first plant dedicated to the transportation market, owned by Applied LNG Technologies or ALT for short. Let's trace the history leading up to the launch and evolution of ALT.

Jack B. Kelley, Inc. was a founder-named company formed in the wake of World War II that first sold helium for balloons and other uses. Helium is extracted, purified and stored using techniques that require a deep knowledge of extremely cold conditions. By the 1960s, Jack Kelley was the country's leading trucker hauling such cryogenically cold products. When he died in 1980, the business passed on to his children.

The Kelley family concluded that the cancer that killed Jack was related to inhaling diesel fumes. This shook them up to the point that they decided to set out on a mission and find a solution that would allow them to continue trucking without the health risks. Ken Kelley, the only son, took over the company's reins as CEO and discovered that he could convert his trucks over to run on LNG instead of diesel using engines and storage tanks that replaced the diesel tanks ubiquitous on 18-wheel tractor trailers.

Kelley also needed a readily available source of LNG and wound up speaking with ExxonMobil, which owned a natural gas processing plant in southwest Wyoming called Schute Creek. Schute Creek's main business was processing natural gas from nearby wells to make it clean enough to be piped downstream and sold on the open market. The

Ken Kelley
Photo credit: Ken Kelley

natural gas running through the Schute Creek plant also contained a small amount of the valuable byproduct, helium. Of course, this is the same product Ken's father sold when he started the family business.

Extracting the helium for sale meant that ExxonMobil was already chilling a stream of gases down to helium's liquefaction temperature of −452 degrees Fahrenheit so it could be separated from the other gases in the mixture. By cooling to this low, low temperature, ExxonMobil was already generating LNG at (the comparatively warm) −260 degrees F. They just hadn't thought seriously about extracting and recovering the LNG until Ken Kelley came along and offered to buy it to run his trucks.

Soon after he started fueling his own trucks with the LNG from Schute Creek, Ken took a call from a representative at Los Angeles International Airport who wanted LNG fuel for forty buses. In short order, the company Applied LNG Technologies – ALT – was born. ALT started rather simply with Ken and his team supplying the fuel from Schute Creek and using portable LNG containers and dispensers that allowed the natural gas to be pumped into

LAX's buses. Thus, the Kelley family's involvement in LNG evolved from a mission ignited by their interest to avenge their patron's death to becoming a torch carrier for a whole new industry.

Almost simultaneously, two energy thought leaders were developing a concept to create an LNG truck fueling corridor. They envisioned this corridor would have refueling stations every 200–300 miles and would run from southern California up Interstate 15 through Las Vegas and on to Salt Lake City, then bend back through Reno to Sacramento on I-80 and down the spine of California on I-5. One of these experts, Cliff Gladstein, was a consultant focused on energy and air pollution issues working from an office in California. The other was Jon Lear, a lawyer and alternative energy strategist from Salt Lake City.

Both Gladstein and Lear had seen the promise and demise of methanol fuels as a clean, low-cost replacement for gasoline in the late 1970s and early 1980s. Methanol can be a great alternative for gasoline. Its quality and performance are so high, in fact, that it's used in Indianapolis race cars. Based on the promise, the state of California supported a grand experiment during the '80s involving methanol fuel. The state donated millions of dollars to each of the major auto manufacturers to convert thousands of cars to run on methanol, or ethanol or mixtures of fuels like the so-called Flexible Fuel vehicles available today. That also enabled start-up companies like Future Fuels of America to begin to convert everyday passenger cars to run on methanol and build stations for refueling.

Unfortunately, the auto manufacturers weren't particularly warm to the idea of methanol fuel, fearing for example that it would eat away at rubber and metal parts in the fuel system. As such, they all ended up deciding not to build significant numbers of methanol-fueled vehicles.* Instead, they supported the use of a methanol-derived

* In the end, only twenty thousand were built.

product called methyl tertiary butyl ether (MTBE for short) that was more compatible with the cars and could easily be blended into gasoline. After growing furiously in the 1990s, the use of MTBE died due to numerous spills that contaminated underground water supplies and because of reported cases of consumer health problems. Gladstein and Lear both foresaw natural gas, specifically LNG, as a better alternative.

In 1996, at a meeting put together by the Texas Railroad Commission, Ken Kelley gave a speech describing his LNG efforts and proposing an LNG fueling corridor for long-distance truckers. By coincidence, Gladstein and Lear were in the audience. They came up to speak with Kelley after his talk and, together, they would become leading proponents for LNG and the truck fueling corridor concept.

To implement their dream, Gladstein's firm founded the Interstate Clean Transportation Corridor, or more succinctly the ICTC. Government agencies jumped on board the ICTC concept for a variety of reasons. Key among these reasons was the reduction in emissions of nitrogen oxides that cause smog and sooty particles that further foul the air and cause health problems. The Federal government was especially keen to halt the deteriorating air quality in the western U.S. that was, among other things, creating visibility problems for visitors to the Grand Canyon and the west's other stunning parks. The California state government jumped on board because air quality in some parts of the state was the worst in the country and among the poorest worldwide. Government funding soon followed.

Private companies also began to support the corridor concept and take stakes in its development. The freight delivery firm UPS, a small supermarket chain headquartered in Sacramento named Raleys and a cattle ranch and beef processor located mid-way between Sacramento and Los Angeles known as Harris Ranch all agreed to convert trucks and host fueling stations. A small number of LNG-fueled trucks were put into fleet service as part of the ICTC. These projects continued into the new millennium but they didn't flourish and the ICTC is only now being fully built out nearly twenty years later.

One of the more significant problems for the early adopters of LNG in the southwest U.S. was simply how far away the market was from Schute Creek. Kelley was instrumental in solving this problem as we will discuss next.*

†††

El Paso Natural Gas owned the Mojave Pipeline, which took natural gas from source wells throughout the Rockies, transported it across the Arizona-California border and, from there, into central California. In the 1990s, El Paso wanted to extend the Mojave Pipeline further northward into the densely populated areas of northern California. Unfortunately for them, the state of California's Public Utilities Commission put up roadblocks. To counter this, El Paso then tried to get approvals to install an LNG liquefier in Bakersfield, so that they could at least nibble around the edges of the central and northern California natural gas market. Anyone who's attempted to build any sort of large facility in California could have predicted the difficulty El Paso would have obtaining the necessary permits and eventually El Paso gave up on the Bakersfield site.

After abandoning Bakersfield, El Paso followed a path of lesser resistance: they decided to build the LNG plant on their pipeline in Arizona, virtually a stone's throw across the California border in a small town called Topock. Arizona was far friendlier at the time to the concept of hosting an

---

* While other LNG plants existed, for most their sole purpose was to convert natural gas to LNG during warm months so it could be stored and then revaporized during the coldest winter days and sent back down pipelines to ensure that schools, hospitals, nursing homes and others could keep the heat on.

LNG production plant than was California, even though interests in California were anxious to use the LNG.

The Topock LNG plant
Photo credit: Ken Kelley

Ken Kelley offered up ALT as the marketer of the product coming from the Topock plant. In so doing, he took on a big gamble because the LNG market was so new, unproven and still very small. The gamble took on the form of a "take-or-pay" agreement between ALT and El Paso. This agreement meant that ALT had rights to buy the product but, in return, either had to take it all or pay for whatever it didn't take. Ken and his company thus had to scramble to convince prospective customers to convert over from tried-and-true diesel to something fairly unproven, or risk big losses. The term of ALT's take-or-pay contract was 10 years, a long time for that sort of a deal under those sorts of circumstances.

It wasn't that easy to convince prospective customers to convert to LNG. The deal Ken struck gave him the rights to the LNG at the plant for about $0.32 per gallon, which, after taking into account the differences in energy density, was like getting if for $0.50 per diesel gallon equivalent.

After hauling the LNG to Los Angeles, for example, the cost of the LNG was maybe $0.75 per diesel gallon equivalent. That was low enough that ALT could sell it for well below the then-current diesel price of about $1.50 per gallon and still turn a profit. On the surface, the cost savings might have looked attractive, but that wasn't the case underneath the surface.

The customers, after all, were unfamiliar with LNG. On top of that, they had to pay big premiums for LNG-capable trucks and buses that were built one-by-one using exotic natural gas engine and storage tank technology versus what they paid for conventional diesel trucks rolling off assembly lines. They also had to put in LNG refueling stations or be able to drive on their routes to new third-party stations which, themselves, contained a significant amount of new technology that was not immune to teething pains. There were also added maintenance costs to make sure the trucks kept running. The fleet maintenance manager and crew had to contend with all this new 'stuff', and contending meant that the usual 5:00 or 6:00 PM clocking-out time quickly became pretty unusual.

Government incentives provided by the state of California to truck and bus fleets helped stimulate the market to some extent. But, Ken had better luck in the initial years selling to companies that used large amounts of LNG for heating and steam production where the economics penciled out more favorably. His first customers included a cookie maker and a wheel manufacturer in northern Mexico, as well as greenhouses operating in the region.

†††

Meanwhile, another effort to produce LNG locally started brewing in Ken Kelley's home state of Texas, which was such a strong bastion of oil industry power that it used to be said that people bled oil.

The Texas legislature was pushing for change in the early 1990s and passed a law that required government fleets to convert over to alternative fuels. This law demanded a ramping up of the fleet's use of alternative fuels, from thirty percent of their total in 1993, to forty percent in 1994 and so on, until they needed to be all-in by the year 2000.

The government-run bus fleet in Texas's largest city, Houston Metro, decided to fulfill this mandate by converting buses over to LNG. Houston Metro hired a company called Stewart & Stevenson to begin to convert the buses over in Denver and also located a source of LNG across the state border at a facility in Lake Charles, LA that was importing LNG. This import terminal was, at the time, only one of two operating. At the terminal, LNG from the Caribbean and northern Africa was brought in by ship and stored in big dock-side tanks, later to be warmed and vaporized, then injected into pipelines and sent to the Midwest, northeast and wherever else it was needed.*

The LNG from Lake Charles provided several advantages for Houston Metro. First, it was always available because the storage system there was huge and always filled with at least some LNG. Second, it was close to Houston, a relatively easy 300 mile round trip (even closer than Topock to Los Angeles). Third, the imported LNG was inexpensive. However, the technology to use LNG was still in its infancy and not all of the problems that cropped up were anticipated, even though they could perhaps have been in hindsight.

The biggest problem Houston Metro encountered involved the impurities in the LNG. These were not impurities in a fuel the way we'd normally think of them, like dirt or water in a gasoline tank, but instead other hydrocarbons besides methane that were present in small amounts. The chief problem is ethane, which has two carbon atoms and six hydrogen atoms (i.e., C_2H_6) to methane's one carbon and four hydrogen's (CH_4). Ethane burns much hotter than methane and too much ethane and too little methane

---

* Two other LNG import terminals had also been built, but were mothballed at the time.

in LNG will quickly burn out an engine, causing thrown rods through engine blocks and other major failures.

The engineers working on the bus conversions did do their homework and concluded rightly that the LNG at Lake Charles was fine for the engines being used. What they didn't anticipate was that somewhere between Lake Charles and the engines, the fuel became richer and richer in ethane. Just like the carbon dioxide that causes fizz in a bottle of soda will eventually escape and leave the soda flat, methane in LNG will gradually vaporize off much faster than ethane, so the LNG can become too high in ethane. This process, called LNG weathering, is inevitable unless controlled by design up front and properly managed on an ongoing basis.

So, the time from when truckers picked up the LNG at Lake Charles and brought it to Houston Metro, then put it in the station's tanks and dispensed it into the buses' fuel tanks, it was gradually increasing in ethane. Then, while the buses were laid up for the weekend, the ethane levels increased even higher. As a result, when the bus drivers started their routes on Mondays, there was often Hell to pay.

A solution was forthcoming in the decision by a company called Liquid Carbonic (owned by another firm, Chicago Bridge & Iron) to build an LNG plant in Willis, TX, 60 miles north of Houston. Liquid Carbonic's main business was cleaning gases up and cooling them down; they were, in fact, a large producer of carbon dioxide in this way. Liquid Carbonic built a plant essentially the same size and design as the one at Topock. This plant was able to maintain ethane in the product below levels where weathering would pose a problem. This was all well and good from a technical point of view.

Unfortunately, due to the earlier experiences of Houston Metro and the desire of other local government fleets not to have to deal with headaches from *their* own alternative fuel teething pains, the Texas legislature decided that the definition of alternative fuels should be amended to

The Willis LNG plant
Photo credit: Ken Kelley

include "reformulated gasoline" and "clean diesel". This change, of course, greatly simplified the work needed for fleets to comply with the law. So, Houston Metro got out of LNG and went back to using diesel.*

With Houston Metro now out of LNG, the plant at Willis became a white elephant. Liquid Carbonic closed the plant down but in effect "left the lights on", a process known as mothballing, so that it could be restarted if ever and whenever it was again needed. The "whenever" happened in the late 1990s after the Liquid Carbonic company was sold by its parent company, CB&I, to another industrial gases company, Praxair. Praxair had no real interest in LNG at the time (although they did build an LNG plant in Brazil in the mid-2000s), but Ken Kelley entered the picture at Willis much like he had at Topock.

As mentioned earlier, Ken Kelley's father had started up his company by selling helium and the Kelley family had held onto this business. Being in perpetually short supply in the U.S. and around the world, helium was (and

---

* Houston Metro is finally again dipping its toe back in the natural gas fuels water now.

remains) very valuable to companies like Praxair, who are among the largest companies sourcing and selling it. Ken was negotiating to sell the family's helium business to Praxair and asked them to throw the Willis plant into the deal for a value of $5 million. Praxair consented, leaving Kelley's ALT business with ownership of the LNG from two plants, the one in Topock and the other in Willis. Ken was the King of LNG.

Of course, a production plant does little good without buyers and, like at Topock, ALT had to begin actively selling the LNG from Willis. They did have some success, supplying LNG to bus fleets in Dallas, Austin and El Paso that didn't have the bad history with LNG that Houston Metro had. We'll return to the story of ALT in Chapter 4.

3

"She Blinded me with Science"
(Thomas Dolby)

s we've seen, the nascent LNG fueling industry during the 1990s was centered in the west and reliant on a few regional plants. Nearly one hundred other LNG plants were also running, but these were used almost exclusively for "peak shaving". That meant they would store large amounts of natural gas in liquid form and release it down the pipeline during severe cold spells. The utilities that owned these plants were not of a mind to upset the local order by taking some of the fuel they were permitted to use for peak shaving and divert it to use as a vehicle fuel. Even if they asked for approval to do this, the regulators in charge probably wouldn't have let them for fear of running out of gas to heat hospitals, schools, nursing homes and the like. So, few people actually considered trying to develop an LNG vehicle fuel market despite the large amounts of fuel that could have been made available. Innovation was needed.

In stepped the government and the natural gas industry's think tanks and research organizations. One of these research organizations, the Gas Technology Institute (GTI), was focused on finding the gaps in the natural gas supply chain and filling them. Their interest spanned how to produce natural gas more economically, pipeline it safely, and make its use more attractive in order to expand the market. One set of researchers and strategists at GTI and another at the Department of Energy's Brookhaven National Labs saw the writing on the wall and decided to work on developing technologies that would let prospective LNG users make the liquid fuel from pipeline gas or landfill gas and fuel as few as several dozen trucks or buses right at the same location.

Funded with assistance from industry allies, GTI and Brookhaven succeeded in piecing together gas cleanup and liquefaction equipment that was so portable it could be loaded on the back of a few pick-up trucks, get transported and rolled into place on a concrete pad, connected to a gas source and be quickly up and running to produce fuel-grade LNG. This system was stepped up to 1,000 gallons per day and then 5,000 gallons per day, enough for between 50 and 100 trucks or buses.

By the early 2000s, the "GTI small-scale LNG liquefier" technology was technically proven and almost ready for commercial use. GTI went out looking for a partner to commercialize it. The industrial gases company BOC (later absorbed by Linde) was out looking for small-scale LNG technology to license and the two organizations struck a deal. By the late 2000s, Linde had deployed a few such systems in Australia using pipeline gas and in Altamont, California using landfill gas. (See Chapter 7 for more on the latter.)

Only a small number of small-scale LNG plants have been built and the technology has not had a major impact on the LNG business, as hoped when GTI and Brookhaven started down this path. On the other hand, it paved the way for others like GE, who still see the benefits of this approach and so are pursuing variants on the small-scale liquefier concept today.

4

"Goin' South"
(Lagwagon)

T he relationship between El Paso and Ken Kelley involving the Topock plant went relatively smoothly until the turn of the millennium. About that time, Enron Corporation was finding ways to game energy markets and one of those efforts involved natural gas supplied to the California market. Enron was able to manipulate prices so that a fixed volume of one thousand cubic feet (MCF) of natural gas ended up in that market at about $10–12. While El Paso did nothing wrong, they benefitted from Enron's actions because they, too, were able to complete sales with natural gas customers in California at that $10–12 per MCF price level. Meanwhile, their deal with ALT was fixed at a sale price of $4 per MCF. Since El Paso could only push so much gas through the pipeline at Topock and into California, every MCF of natural gas the company sold to ALT at the lower price was at the expense of sales at the higher price to others and that was costing them profits.

According to Kelley, El Paso called 'force majeure' and shut down the plant when prices went up like this, depriving ALT of the LNG that they needed to resell to its customers. Force majeure is a legal term that essentially means "something has gone terribly wrong and we can't supply you with what we agreed to." (Generally, force majeure is invoked when there's a catastrophic, unplanned breakdown of something in a plant or weather that prevents deliveries.) Since ALT was on the hook to make its deliveries to customers relying on them, Kelley and his team worked overtime to get product to ALT's customers from Schute Creek, WY and even, when necessary, from

ALT LNG transport truck
Photo credit: Ken Kelley

as far away as Willis, TX. The drive from Schute Creek to Los Angeles is a thirty hour round-trip, versus eight hours round trip from Topock to Los Angeles and ALT was unable to pass along the extra freight cost to its customers.* The costs to ALT were high. Frustrated, Kelley filed a lawsuit against El Paso for breach of contract.

Ken Kelley also struggled to sell out more than twenty percent of what the Willis plant could produce during the early 2000s. His siblings, who were not as warm to the LNG business, put pressure on him to sell ALT, including the Topock and Willis plants, and get back to running the family business hauling other companies' products around. In 2005, he did.

Actually, Kelley made several deals to unravel his position in LNG. The lawsuit with El Paso was settled, by which he received both a cash settlement of $25 million and ownership of Topock. Kelley then sold ALT to a company called Apollo Resources., which then re-formed under the name Earth Biofuels.

In buying ALT's business, Earth Biofuels became an interesting amalgamation of a biodiesel supplier that sold

---

* Some LNG was also available to ALT from another plant in southwest Colorado.

product into the diesel marketplace and an LNG supplier that competed directly with diesel. Earth Biofuels was a publicly traded company and its President and CEO Dennis McLaughlin enlisted well-known personalities to help sell its story, among them the actors Julia Roberts and Morgan Freeman, singer Willie Nelson and NASCAR driver Rusty Wallace. Reportedly, one wag dubbed the company the "'Planet Hollywood' of alternative energy stocks", while reports emerged about missed debt payments, enlisting of penny stock shills and flawed expansion into the ethanol fuels market.

In the end, the star aura didn't help save Earth Biofuels. McLaughlin ran afoul of creditors and in June 2008 the LNG business was sold to the newly-formed PNG Ventures, another over-the-counter stock company that was in fact largely owned by Earth Biofuels' creditors. Given the difficulties ALT and then Apollo and Earth Biofuels had in growing the LNG business, plus the subsequent financial problems of PNG, McLaughlin's assertion at the time that the "imputed value" of the transaction was $125 million seems a bit optimistic.*

Within a few years, PNG also had financial problems, and was resold to creditors, yet again reemerging under the name Applied LNG Technologies. The remaining pieces of Earth Biofuels, including biodiesel and ethanol, were renamed Evolution Energy, but that company ultimately died too, with creditors and shareholders left holding the bag.

Kelley also separately shopped the Willis plant around to potential buyers who, he hoped, would see the unfulfilled potential of the LNG market much like he did. In the end, that buyer was Kelley's competitor, Clean Energy Fuels, who paid $15 million for the plant and continues to own and run it today.

* For more information, see: http://www.fool.com/investing/high-growth/2007/01/03/earth-biofuels-kiss-of-death.aspx and http://www.bizjournals.com/dallas/stories/2008/06/09/daily30.html.

5

"The Rising"
(Bruce Springsteen)

T. Boone Pickens' company, Clean Energy Fuels, continued to grow quickly during the early 2000s, increasing from $20 million in sales in 2002 to over $90 million in 2006. Pickens and others funded much of this growth with loans, the balance with equity stakes from companies like Westport Innovations (the natural gas equipment manufacturer) and Terasen Gas (the new name of the British Columbia natural gas utility that had owned BCG Fuels). Aside from adding LNG and CNG fueling stations to its portfolio, Clean Energy struck the deal with Ken Kelley to buy ALT's Willis, Texas LNG plant in 2005. This was a win-win: a good deal for Ken given that he had bought it for $5 million and sold it for $15 million, but also well below what a comparable new plant would have cost.

Clean Energy decided it would be propitious to float an Initial Public Offering (IPO) in 2007 to spur additional growth, make investments that didn't require funding from Pickens and other early investors, and to create a market for their stock so those investors could cash out. Pickens and others had been acquiring shares and stock options and warrants (rights to buy shares) in Clean Energy before the IPO at prices as low as $2.96 per share, so they stood to gain significantly given the initial offering price of $12.00 per share.

In its filing prospectus, Clean Energy summarized the reasons why natural gas fuels make sense: cheaper, cleaner-burning and domestically available. These justifications have held up consistently during the emergence of these fuels. By becoming the first American company specifically focused solely on the CNG and LNG fuel supply space to go public, Clean Energy wanted to be able to pull away from ALT (which still owned the plant at Topock, Arizona), Trillium and others in the market.

Hoping to raise $137 million in its IPO, Clean Energy's main three goals were to fund an LNG plant in California, build over $30 million of CNG and LNG fueling stations, and buy several hundred heavy-duty trucks that could be supplied to customers in order to be a one-stop shop: supply the trucks, the fuel and the locations to refuel. The sale of 10 million shares of stock at $12.00 was completed in June 2007 and the company netted $108 million after expenses.

So far, investing in Clean Energy stock at the IPO price and just holding on to it since 2007 wouldn't have yielded much different results than stuffing money in a mattress; investing in a basket of Dow Jones, S&P 500 or NASDAQ stocks would have yielded better returns. The company has had to continue issuing more shares to continue growing, effectively diluting the per-share price of anybody who already owned stock.*

Clean Energy's plan to build an LNG plant in California was already well underway by the time of the IPO. In 2005, Clean Energy struck a deal with U.S. Borax to locate the plant on a corner of their property in Boron, California. U.S. Borax was mining and processing boron salts in the high desert about 120 miles northeast of Los Angeles and the location was ideal for Clean Energy because it was remote enough to facilitate permitting (which is what had tripped up El Paso in Bakersfield a decade earlier), close enough to Los Angeles to make easy work of hauling the product to the heart of the LNG market at the time, and located on a major interstate pipeline where the feed gas could be efficiently liquefied.

Clean Energy's Boron LNG plant was designed to supply the existing and potentially much larger future California

---

* The total number of shares outstanding as of this writing is nearly 90 million, versus 10 million shares initially.

LNG market. Enormously important to the future demand side was a statewide referendum, Proposition 1B, passed in November 2006. The full name was "Proposition 1B: The Highway Safety, Traffic Reduction, Air Quality, and Port Security Bond Act", but generally referred to simply as Prop. 1B.

Prop 1B allowed for about $20 billion of spending on infrastructure around the state, including $2 billion of grants from the state and local agencies to businesses under California's Goods Movement Emission Reduction Program. An anticipated cornerstone of the $2 billion of spending was expected to be the conversion to LNG of many of the sixteen thousand heavy-duty trucks that haul imported goods out of the ports of Los Angeles and Long Beach. Clean Energy was a major supporter of Prop 1B and expected that perhaps one-third to one-half of those trucks would use LNG, especially LNG from their new plant in Boron.

Clean Energy pushed hard for these truck conversions to occur and built a large LNG fueling station at the mouth of the Port of Long Beach to support them. At the time, however, there was significant pushback by independent truckers, some of whom owned only one or a handful of trucks, who were concerned about the high cost of buying the new trucks. In fact, a more general controversy was underway about whether truckers were receiving "living wages", meaning wages high enough to live on above subsistence levels.

Since a new LNG truck might cost $40,000–100,000 more than a new diesel-fueled truck, most truckers who needed to make an investment opted to buy clean diesel trucks instead. In the end, well less than 1,000 new LNG trucks were bought at the time to serve the southern California ports. This created much lower demand than anticipated and since Clean Energy was sharing this market with ALT's Topock plant, demand for LNG from Boron fell far short of the 160,000 gallons per day of the plant's capacity. The plant remained under-utilized for some time.

6

"The Trip to Bountiful"
(The Adventures)

J ust as there was slow, often sideways, progress with LNG, so too did CNG bump along, taking a step back for every two steps forward during the 1990s and 2000s. Some taxi, bus and trash truck fleets made large investments in CNG vehicles, but an important prize – shifting part of America's three hundred million passenger cars – remained elusive.

To get enough natural gas into a car or light-duty truck for practical use, you need to compress it up to at least a few thousand psi. Right now, the standard is 3,600 psi, which is two hundred forty times the pressure and density if the gas were floating free in the atmosphere, just high enough to get five to ten or so gallons worth of fuel into a vehicle's tank. Pressurizing the natural gas is not a difficult thing to do, although you also have to make sure to dry the pipeline gas before compressing it and you also have to then make sure to use a well-designed fuel dispenser connector that fits securely into the fuel tank inlet, unlike a gasoline dispenser nozzle that simply fits loosely into the mouth of the gas tank.

A complete basic (fast-fill) CNG refueling station can be bought and installed for less than a million dollars (and perhaps as low as $600,000 as of this writing), which is not too expensive if you then also have enough vehicles using it to justify the investment.* But, there just haven't been many vehicle choices available to potential CNG car buyers until recently. Honda began selling a CNG-fueled

---

* Newly-designed and novel CNG stations can now be bought for far less than this amount and in-home CNG refueling "appliances" discussed later may wind up costing as little as $500 or so.

Civic in 1998 and this has proved to be a relatively popular, albeit niche, product. Meanwhile, Ford helped oversee a significant number of Crown Victoria conversions to CNG. But, the Crown Vic was a niche product to begin with (save for some police and taxi fleets) and sales declined since around the year 2000, so Ford saw no incentive to keep the CNG variant around.

Many consumers hired out the conversion of their own cars and trucks to shops that would install CNG tanks and controls, typically while leaving in the gasoline tanks as well. This was not always a well-regulated approach and it wasn't unusual to see these fiberglass-wrapped CNG tanks bolted into the backs of SUVs and pick-ups where the valves, and the tanks themselves, were susceptible to getting banged up.

†††

Perhaps the most intriguing consumer CNG passenger car market in the 2000s was in Utah around the cities of Salt Lake City, Provo and Ogden, where somewhere close to 10,000 such cars were running. There, the local gas utility Questar had installed close to 20 CNG stations in the wake of EPACT.

The Questar stations had been maintained and serviceable, but were clearly under-powered to fuel many cars and pick-ups (as well as heavy-duty tractor trailer trucks that used them). Standing at one of these, you could see dynamics similar to many of the EPACT stations, as cars or light-duty trucks would come in and begin fueling, getting all of maybe five gasoline gallons worth of CNG on-board in five or ten minutes. Then, as before, because of the stations' design limitations, a second vehicle would pull up after the first and likely take ten or fifteen minutes to fill, while a third might well take over twenty minutes.

Compounding this long time to refuel, drivers typically had to go out of their way to get to the stations because of the limited number covering a large metropolitan area.

Plus, the CNG stations sometimes broke down, meaning that drivers then had to drive even further to get to the next available working station.

Even obtaining cars like the Civic or a converted Chevy Cavalier often meant tracking one down for sale in California (since they weren't available new locally) and driving it back to Utah. People put up with it because the cost of the fuel was only about $1 per gallon. You'd often hear drivers, standing next to their vehicles while the CNG dribbled in, say that they planned their days around refueling and often had to do so every day because of the small tanks and incomplete refills. In spite of the problems, most everyone who had a CNG car or truck in Utah loved the cost savings enough so they swore by natural gas fuel (and not at it).

†††

Besides the grassroots use of CNG in personal autos by individuals, Clean Energy Fuels and a few other companies competed tooth-and-nail for business with municipal bus and taxi fleets to let them install stations at their depots and central fueling hubs such as airports and thus become their exclusive CNG suppliers. One of these companies was Trillium USA, noted earlier.* Trillium gave Clean Energy Fuels a run for the money as a builder, owner and operator of large stations for CNG fleets, vying for business especially with customers in California.

While Clean Energy Fuels and Trillium vied for the service end of the CNG fleet business by owning and operating stations for customers, other companies served the needs of customers who simply wanted to buy the stations to own and operate themselves. Chief among these has been ANGI

* Trillium and its sister company, Pinnacle CNG Systems were bought in 2011 for $50 million by Integrys Energy Group, a public natural gas and electric power utility company, during the recent surge of interest in NGVs.

and IMW (now owned by Clean Energy), but there were numerous other competitors. Essentially, any company that could engineer and package a compressor together with the rest of the system components or any company that built compressors suitable to be used for CNG could have packaged the other pieces with compressors (such as dispensers and controls) and entered the CNG station selling business. Many did so as a means to diversify.

This dichotomous set of options for consumers: buy the CNG from another company that has installed the station or buy the station and run it yourself is where the battle for the hearts, minds and wallets of truck, bus and car (e.g., taxi) fleet consumers will be fought out. (See Chapter 24.)

7

"Waste it All"

(Kim Williams-Smith)

The early natural gas fuels business often developed as a result of unusual circumstances, ironically including the efforts of an oil man, T. Boone Pickens, who later championed natural gas. Some of the early significant users of natural gas came from unexpected directions. Among these is Waste Management, whose trash-hauling trucks are found in nearly every corner of the United States.

Waste Management was formed in 1968 by the merger of companies started by a Dutch immigrant, Harry Wayne Huizenga, and Dean Buntrock. Within fifteen years, Waste Management grew to become the largest trash company in the U.S., hauling refuse from homes and businesses and dumping it in landfills. By the late 1990s the company, now called WMX, was at the lead of a rapidly consolidating waste industry. But, it then became embroiled in several accounting scandals. The company ultimately emerged from these debacles bruised and battered, but able to again pick up the gauntlet and continue growing.

At about the same time that these indiscretions had garnered so much attention, the company started making bold moves in alternative fuels by using trash collection trucks outfitted with natural gas engines. The initial tests didn't always go smoothly and the company still had teething pains even after more than ten years. However, they stuck with it and now the company has over two thousand natural gas-fueled heavy-duty trucks, presently the largest such fleet in the country.

One of Waste Management's early tests involved fueling with LNG in southwest Pennsylvania at their Washington facility. The history of that effort traces back to as early as 1991 when the Washington, PA facility's previous owners tried to figure out how to use the gas from its landfill as fuel. Landfill gas can be up to one-half methane, but it also has large amounts of carbon dioxide, which doesn't burn, and hundreds of other compounds that can create noxious and corrosive byproducts when burned. Largely due to the complex mix of contaminants, neither the original landfill's owners nor WM who later acquired it concluded that the landfill gas could be put to beneficial use economically with the technology available at the time.

WM next considered the use of pipeline CNG to fuel its trucks. After careful analysis, the people working on the project concluded that by the time they added CNG tanks to the collection trucks, the extra weight would cut into how much trash the trucks could hold, making it unfeasible for them to complete their pick-up rounds. The solution to this dilemma came in the form of LNG. Since LNG is over two times as dense as CNG, they could pack more LNG on board with relatively light tanks that allowed them to drive for up to 13 hours and therefore didn't impede the core business of collecting the trash. WM and a consortium of government laboratories, private organizations and partners took baby steps in this direction by testing LNG-fueled trucks supplied by Mack and installing an LNG fueling station on-site to fuel them.

While promising, the Washington, PA LNG trial wasn't economically self-sustaining, as the technology was too immature and the operating costs were simply too high.

However, within a few years, WM began testing LNG trucks in California. This program had more traction, encouraged not only by the economics but also by pressure being brought to bear from the California state government to reduce smog and improve air quality, which in turn steered municipalities to encourage their waste hauling contractors to use at least some natural gas trucks. Given that the cargo involved was trash, a nice added benefit of the LNG trucks was ironically that there was no diesel smell. As a consequence, WM started touting that their drivers' wives (generally the drivers were men) were happier when their husbands came home from work. Also, natural gas-fueled trucks run much quieter than diesel trucks with their knocking and chugging sounds.* That's a nice bonus for customers who might otherwise be awakened by the garbage truck making its early morning rounds through their neighborhoods, even though it didn't solve the problem of banging garbage cans and dumpsters.

Based on its initial successes, WM began buying LNG-fueled trucks and building stations across southern California during the early-to-mid 2000s. Furthermore, the company added to its count of natural gas fueled trucks as it bought up existing waste hauling companies that had already begun to convert their fleets.

The undertaking was still not devoid of problems. Perhaps chief among these concerned the storage tanks that held the LNG on the sides of the trucks. Recall that LNG is naturally very cold, so it warms up and vents off if left sitting for too long. Some of the storage tanks that were sold at the time were defective so the LNG boiled off far more quickly than it should have.

The tanks weren't defective straight out of the box, so they passed inspections at their point of manufacture. However, the insulating material that was used in the vacuum between the tank walls wasn't properly packed in, so as the trucks gradually accumulated miles rumbling down the road, the insulation settled down the sides exposing large areas that lost their insulating properties. The LNG had no defense against warming from the often-hot California weather and was lost forever into the atmosphere.

---

* Diesel engines are, by nature, "compression ignition" engines, which means that for every cycle a piston undergoes, there is a small physical explosion in that cylinder. In contrast, the expansion in the cylinders is gentler in "spark-ignited" engines, so the noise is far lower.

Just as Houston Metro had experienced years before, drivers would get in their trucks after weekends and find their fuel tanks empty, which of course caused headaches and wasted time as the trucks had to be towed to the other end of the yard and refueled. More importantly, the loss of fuel showed up as a costly operating loss. What was the point of using a fuel that was one-third less expensive per gallon when you'd lose the benefit if, say, one-third of your fuel evaporated into thin air?

Even though WM was able to open up the defective tanks, add new insulation and re-vacuum ("re-vac") them, the headaches that WM was having with LNG were reason enough at the time to add more CNG-fueled trucks to the fleet instead of more LNG trucks. In addition, CNG was certainly less expensive than LNG. On top of that, CNG tank technology had advanced significantly since the 1990s, so that more fuel could be stored on board and WM was also able to plan its fleet operations to suit each fuel, sending LNG trucks out each day on long routes and CNG trucks out for shorter routes.

All of these LNG and CNG fueling efforts allowed Waste Management to save money, reduce emissions and tout its "green-ness" compared with diesel, but the company had further ambitions that echoed the original intent in Washington, PA to use gas from the landfill. Technologies to clean up landfill gas had advanced significantly, so WM now had the choice of producing "renewable" CNG or LNG from it. There were trade-offs: At that time (and even now) it was prohibitively expensive to transport large quantities of CNG on board a trailer to be able to ship it from the landfill to a fueling station located somewhere else; it needed to be used on-site. So, the size of a renewable CNG project was limited by the number of trucks stopping at that landfill. By comparison, as much LNG could be produced at a landfill as decomposition of the organic matter in the landfill would allow. The LNG could then be economically shipped to trash collection truck depots elsewhere.

Waste Management decided to go in the direction of renewable LNG, in effect going big and bold. They started working with a start-up company called CryoFuel Systems that had developed a technology that would, it was claimed, economically clean up the landfill gas to LNG-grade methane and chill it down to LNG temperatures. Ken Kelley was also involved in this effort and he had already begun working with CryoFuel to build the first such commercial plant in Irvine, California. WM and Kelley together invested several million dollars in CryoFuel, which failed to deliver the goods, leaving WM and Kelley holding the bag.

WM didn't give up, however. They began to work with a spin-off of CryoFuel Systems named CryoEnergy International, which had acquired some of the rights to CryoFuel's technology. Like with CryoFuel, the intent of WM and CryoEnergy to develop a commercial renewable LNG plant again didn't pan out. WM moved on yet again and in this case was able to successfully develop a commercial-scale renewable LNG plant at WM's Altamont, California landfill with the German-owned company, Linde. The Altamont plant can supply up to about 300 garbage collection trucks daily around the state.*

Waste Management continues to use some conventional and some renewable LNG in California, along with CNG. In its other operations, WM has chosen to concentrate exclusively on using CNG. The company has further broken new ground by broadly supporting the use of so-called "time-fill CNG" stations, where every driver can pull his or her truck into a parking spot, connect a hose to

---

* Meantime, the founders of CryoFuel Systems started up a new company named Prometheus Energy that went ahead and built the renewable LNG plant in Irvine. After spending tens of millions of dollars on that project, multiple times the original budget, Prometheus abandoned the plant and sold off the pieces. Prometheus still exists and is pursuing other LNG interests.

the compression system and leave it overnight to fill at a trickle, returning the next morning to a full tank.

WM's major competitors in the waste industry have also jumped into CNG fueling to remain competitive and have even dabbled in renewable natural gas fuels. (See Chapter 33 for more information on that product.) Nowadays, nearly fifty percent of all refuse trucks being purchased in the U.S. run on natural gas fuels, and for WM, the percent of such new purchases is around ninety five percent.

8

"Eternal Consumption Engine"
(Primus)

Before the recent surge of interest in natural gas fuels, quite a few big-name companies in the engine and vehicle business tried, and often failed, to create an economically sustainable technology platform to support the natural gas fuels business. By platform, I'm referring to developing reliable natural gas-fueled engines, integrating them with on-board fuel systems, and then further integrating them into vehicle chasses. These efforts were costly, time-consuming and difficult.

The early efforts generally came in the form of tests or trials, so setbacks and failures were to be expected. They were well meaning and typically offered to early adopters in good faith. But, in their enthusiasm to advance and grow the business, suppliers sometimes overpromised performance on the road and reliability and the end result was many unhappy customers.

Suppliers were especially not ready to serve the needs of the most attractive market segment – large truck fleets – which resulted in unmet expectations and consumer frustration here. This actually resulted in setbacks in the goal of establishing a sustainable, healthy and growing industry. It has taken more than a decade to recover from these problems.

†††

Cummins Inc. is one of the largest – perhaps *the* largest-manufacturers of diesel engines in the world and was the first to take natural gas engines seriously enough to introduce a steady stream of new products for natural gas fuels. They've supplied natural gas engines since 1989, introducing an alphabet soup-like series of pure natural gas spark-ignited engine products of various sizes – the L10G, C8.3, C-Plus and ISLG. Each has been an improvement over the previous generation, although the flaws of each generation may not have always been apparent at the time.

In particular, reliability was an ongoing problem into the 2000s. The cause has sometimes been attributed to the fact that natural gas doesn't lubricate piston linings the way diesel can. This lack of lubrication is obvious when you consider methane is a pure gas, while diesel is a mixture of liquids that can create slipperiness. The lack of lubricity can be ameliorated with the right engine metallurgy (or alternatively by using natural gas along with diesel in some type of bi-fuel engine).

Beginning around 2001, Cummins began to market its 6- to 9-liter natural gas engine products for trucks through a joint venture it has with the Vancouver, Canada-based technology company Westport Innovations. Cummins builds these engines and the JV, called Cummins Westport, markets and sells them. Cummins has been too deep into diesel engine products and too uncertain about the future of natural gas fuels to try to directly convince its core customers to use CNG or LNG; the JV was better for that. However, now that the market is becoming better established, Cummins has moved from being a diesel fuel advocate to straddling the diesel-natural gas fuel fence; in fact Cummins will directly market a new 15-liter heavy duty natural gas truck engine in the next few years.

In the mid 1990s, the bulldog-bearing brand Mack Trucks also took steps in the direction of a natural gas fuels product platform by linking up with two private research groups, the Southwest Research Institute and the Gas Research Institute, now the Gas Technology Institute, to develop and test natural gas-based truck engines and the trucks themselves. The remarkable and most forward-thinking aspect about Mack's approach was that they were able to build these trucks right on their diesel truck assembly line. This was done by posting the natural gas equipment spec on the card attached to the engine and truck chassis before it passed into the line. When the engine or chassis reached each assembly station, the worker there knew to put on the natural gas fuel tank, piping and engine parts needed.

†††

The industry took a further turn when, in 1998, the U.S. Environmental Protection Agency slammed the major truck and bus diesel engine manufacturers with over $1 billion in fines and mandated product improvements. The EPA charged them with circumventing air pollution laws by designing and building their engines to be capable of passing emission performance tests before letting them on the road, knowing they'd then become out of compliance once they were put into service. The engine companies denied any wrongdoing but also agreed to the EPA's terms, including speeding up efforts to improve their engines and reduce emissions.

Such product improvements were already scheduled by the EPA, but the settlement reached kick-started radical changes in the actions and positions of the engine companies, and the repercussions are still being felt today. The EPA passed regulations that forced reductions in smog-forming nitrogen oxide emissions and in sooty particulates from engines every few years: 2004, 2007 and 2010. These low emission levels were harder and harder for diesel engines to achieve, although not very difficult for natural gas engines.

In response, Cummins pursued a dual-pronged strategic approach, improving their diesel engine emissions using after-market add-on control devices while also stepping deeper into natural gas.* Having natural gas engines provided Cummins with an important alternative to a diesel-only product line. On the other hand, Caterpillar simply exited the on-road engine business in the U.S.

---

* It costs the engine manufacturers millions of dollars to test every new generation and model of engine, a not-inconsequential sum.

A third leader in the business, International, dug in their heels by refusing to put on after-market devices. Unfortunately, emission limits tightened every few years and by 2010 International had to throw in the towel on diesel-fueled engines in the U.S. Another major engine supplier, Detroit Diesel (owned by Daimler), focused almost exclusively on remaining competitive in diesel, relying on the aftermarket emission controls approach to compete.

Engines that ran on natural gas fuels emerged (and sometimes disappeared) from sources other than the major diesel engine market leaders. For example, a company named Clean Air Power used a technology for blending up to 60–70% natural gas with diesel and had some success with this approach via a partnership with Caterpillar. Clean Air Power sold engines to the freight company UPS around the year 2000 and these engines are still running in UPS's trucks today after some 1,500,000 miles of operation. But, Clean Air Power couldn't easily adapt their engines to the stricter air quality rules that went into effect by 2007 so had to pull out of the U.S. market.

The heavy equipment manufacturer, John Deere, introduced an engine similar in concept to the Cummins products and tried primarily to sell it to buses and a few truck fleets. This engine got very positive reviews by the customers for its high reliability, but Deere pulled out of the market after losing a few large bids, much to the consternation of fleet owners looking for a strong competitor to Cummins.

Meantime, Westport Innovations, the partner selling Cummins' natural gas engines up to 12 liters in size, also plugged along with the design and sales of a 15 liter engine that uses a technology very different from the more ubiquitous spark-ignited natural gas engines. This "high pressure direct injection" (HPDI) engine is explained further in the sidebar and in Chapter 21.

†††

CNG-fueled Truck
Photo credit: Freightliner Corporation

Engines are the core components in natural gas vehicles, so get a lot of attention. But it's the vehicles themselves that must be produced and sold to the public. Like the engines, this has created sticking points affecting growth. The heavy-duty truck market is dominated in the U.S. by a few large original equipment manufacturers (OEMs) like Freightliner (owned by Daimler), Kenworth and Peterbilt (both independently run but owned by a common parent, PACCAR), Mack (owned by the Swedish company Volvo), and Navistar (formerly International). Given the uncertainty of the sustainability of the natural gas fuels vehicle market, it comes as no surprise that these companies sat on the fence – occasionally falling to one side or the other – until recently.

The gap in the sustained availability of heavy-duty natural gas-fueled trucks had to be filled somehow, and that "somehow" has been through independent companies that assemble the engines, fuel systems and controls into the OEMs' truck chasses. The largest of these converters is Agility Fuel Systems, whose history can be traced back to two companies. These companies include a fuel storage expert company FAB Industries (founded in 1996) and an

alternative vehicle systems engineering firm Enviromech
Industries (founded in 2001) that merged in early 2011 to
form Agility.

The three major auto companies Ford, General Motors
and Chrysler sold natural gas cars as far back as the 1980s,
but their commitment also wavered with the waxing and
waning demand. All three exited the U.S. market for NGVs
(while supporting NGV market developments overseas)
and the only company that has stuck it out through this
whole period is Honda. The result is that the market was
sustained largely by small independent companies that
do the conversions using parts assembled from various
sources on cars sourced from the OEMs and individuals.
These converters perform the same function that Agility
Fuel Systems has for heavy-duty trucks: providing technical solutions to meet the needs of consumers, continuing
to breathe life into the market through its ups and downs,
and creating a cottage industry for light-duty natural gas
vehicles.

A Few Words About Engines and Fuels

There are two main types of engines used in vehicles: spark-ignited and compression-ignited. Natural gas can be used in both.

Gasoline, generally used in our cars, is suited to spark-ignited engines. Gasoline has a high octane rating. (That's the rating you see on the side of the pump.) High octane means the fuel is well suited to burning at just the right time and the right amount when a spark plug is lit. Natural gas has a very high octane rating of 120. Such a high rating doesn't necessarily hurt, but it does mean the engine may need to be tweaked. So, a natural gas-fueled car will need the engine controls adjusted as well as have a special tank and piping installed. That's not a lot of differences compared with a gasoline-fueled car. So, the development history of light-duty natural gas fueled vehicles has been relatively straightforward and easy. The main challenge will be increasing the numbers of these vehicles sold so assembly lines can create the same economies of scale as everyday gasoline-fueled cars.

In contrast to cars that generally use gasoline (in this country at least), heavy-duty tractor trailer trucks are almost always equipped with compression-ignited engines that thrive with diesel fuel. These engines are a bit more energy efficient than gasoline-fueled spark-ignited engines and are built to last for hundreds of thousands of miles. Fact is, they last so long because the engines are over-built to withstand the pounding they take every time the fuel is lit. It should be obvious that the fuel in compression-ignited engines ignites when the fuel is compressed. Spark plugs aren't needed because when diesel fuel is injected into the top of an engine's cylinder and the piston rises, it squeezes the fuel, causing it to automatically ignite from the pressure. Diesel is rated by its cetane, not octane, number and this is a measure of how easily diesel fuel ignites upon compression. Natural gas' cetane number is far lower than diesel's; it does not easily ignite by compression. To overcome this, technology for natural gas heavy-duty engines used in tractor trailers (and most ships, locomotives and other high horsepower uses) has taken two tracks. In the first approach, the engine and fuel injection system are modified so a little bit of diesel is squirted into the cylinder to start the ignition under pressure and act like a pilot light. Once the diesel starts the ignition process, natural gas can be flooded into the same chamber, where it also burns and supplies most of the energy. This requires pretty complicated engineering. In the second approach, the manufacturers of the trucks simply order up a high horsepower spark-ignited engine instead of a compression-ignited one, recognizing the truck will be less efficient so will get fewer miles per gallon. However, since spark plugs work well with the high-octane inherent in pure natural gas, this allows for a straight-forward and relatively simple approach to engine design.

9

"Train in Vain"
(The Clash)

The main early efforts with natural gas fuels involved their use in cars and trucks, plus stationary users like those Ken Kelley pursued to help sell out the Topock LNG plant. In addition to those mainstream efforts, there were early experiments to use LNG in applications where the engines are much larger than those found in even the largest trucks. These experiments foreshadowed the more recent revolution in natural gas fuels sparked by other high horsepower LNG fueling markets.

L.A. Junction LNG locomotive
Photo credit: Ken Kelley

One of these programs involved using LNG to power locomotives, the premise being that these tend to be large users of diesel fuel operating in a business where pennies count. Significant efforts around this took place in the 1990s involving trials focused on using natural gas for local runs such as in the Los Angeles area. For instance, the L.A. Junction Railroad used an engine that only ran in the local rail yard. Also, BNSF ran two engines on LNG so they could use emission credits to put an extra diesel locomotive on the trains leaving the L.A. basin that went to Las Vegas.

This effort proved that LNG could be used as a locomotive fuel. But the inherent economics were not compelling, especially as natural gas prices couldn't be counted on at the time to provide enough long-term savings to justify the large investment in fueling and on-board storage required. So, the efforts were shelved. However, these trials did ultimately prove useful later on since some of the equipment used in the first round has been dusted off, checked out, refurbished and reused in the latest round of demonstrations (see Chapter 29).

PART II: 2008–2013

10

"Another Chance at Love"
(Allen Shamblin-Brent Maher, Shelby Lynne)

T he relative stagnation in natural gas fueling during much of the first decade after 2000 would most likely have continued were it not for two events. The first was the radical top-down change in natural gas production technology (involving shale gas, profiled in the sidebar) that has led to high levels of production and systemically low prices, and the second was a nearly simultaneous bottom-up effort to use natural gas fuels in novel ways related to extracting shale gas.

Until the late 2000s, the LNG fueling story in the U.S. revolved mainly around trucks operating in California served by Clean Energy's Boron plant and ALT's Topock plant. Outside of California, there was scattered LNG fuel demand served by Clean Energy's (still underutilized) plant in Willis, TX acquired from ALT and by Schute Creek and Williams' Ignacio, Colorado plants. In the course of a few years, interest in LNG fuel dramatically grew, starting with the efforts of a few companies dabbling in an entirely new area of use for LNG – namely to run drilling rig equipment.

At the same time that LNG was being applied in new ways, momentum was building for CNG, allowing for both fuels to become primed to make the breakthroughs we are now experiencing.

These dynamics have changed radically in the intervening years.

11

"Revolution"
(The Beatles)

S ince the 1990s, the expectation of industry insiders was that more and more taxis, buses and trucks would eventually use CNG and LNG, and that the market would eventually come into its own once there were enough appropriate engines, vehicle chasses and fueling stations at a low enough cost to spur consumer demand. This expectation has been turned on its head by the actions of a few natural gas operating companies (that is the companies that commission well drilling and completion, and own the wells that produce the gas).

These companies' main mission is to produce natural gas, but ironically they were using diesel fuel to power all of their drilling rigs, hydraulic fracturing equipment and large service trucks. This situation was summed up by one gas industry businessman who said "We're like a dairy owner who doesn't drink milk." A few leaders in the natural gas business, notably a Canadian-owned firm with activities also spread through parts of the U.S. named Encana, were the first to realize and act on this irony.

At the time, Encana was one of the top two or three natural gas companies in North America. However, its activities in Canada were significantly larger than in the U.S. and it wasn't as well known as peers such as Chesapeake Energy, Devon Energy and XTO Energy, the latter which was on the verge of being bought by ExxonMobil.*

Several Encana executives saw that spurring new uses of natural gas and driving up the demand side was important to creating profitable growth, especially because the

---

* ExxonMobil announced the acquisition of XTO in 2009 and closed on the deal in 2010.

concurrent revolution in natural gas production techniques was driving up supply. New outlets for natural gas were needed. So, Encana began to experiment with using LNG (and taking the gas from pipelines and nearly straight out of the ground) to fuel large 2,000 horsepower engines that had been modified to use mixtures of natural gas with diesel instead of diesel alone. These initial tests were successful, so Encana took the next step of commissioning the building of large portable equipment that could store the LNG and vaporize it at many well-sites for Encana's drilling operations.

Encana took several further steps to encourage natural gas fuel demand, like striking a deal with a new company, Heckmann Corporation, which was starting to get into the business of hauling water to hydraulic fracturing sites. Encana and Heckmann struck a symbiotic deal: Heckmann received Encana's business hauling water to their rig sites in return for Heckmann agreeing to convert their water hauling truck fleet to fuel with natural gas in the form of LNG. Heckmann thus placed the biggest natural gas-fueled truck order up to that time, two hundred trucks equipped with the largest natural gas-fueled engine available, Westport's 15 liter, 450 horsepower HPDI engine.

So, here we were with Encana, a Canada-based company, taking the bull by the horns to create demand for natural gas fuels in the U.S. by using it for drilling and also incentivizing truckers to convert over to it. This apparently did not sit well with Aubrey McClendon, who was at the helm over at Encana's chief U.S. competitor Chesapeake Energy.

†††

Chesapeake was still only a 20-year old company when the shale gas revolution and Encana's forays into LNG began. The company was started and run by Chairman and CEO Aubrey McClendon, who was perceived by many to be both flamboyant and also possibly the most vocal advocate for the natural gas production industry. Equal parts showman to the investment community, benevolent father figure to his employees and wild-eyed visionary, McClendon was one of the earliest business leaders in America to understand how important shale gas would become. His late-stage tenure at Chesapeake also swirled with controversy as the company became awash in reports about conflicts of interest between the company and McClendon, ethical lapses involving lease holdings and claims of collusion (with Encana) to suppress land lease prices, and debt that swelled to effectively unsustainable levels.

McClendon followed news of Encana's efforts to develop the natural gas fueling market. With Chesapeake being even larger than Encana in the U.S. and with his reputation as chief industry visionary on the line, he decided to make an even bolder statement. McClendon commissioned a high-level team at Chesapeake to identify moves the company could make to radically change the fuel market. He pledged $1 billion of investment money (equal to one-eighth of its revenues in 2009) via a subsidiary, Peake Fuel Solutions, to act as an internal venture capital company to fund this effort. Part of this was set aside to help a start-up company, Sundrop Fuels, develop technology to convert natural gas into petroleum-like substances, while the balance and larger share was expected to help develop natural gas fuels themselves.

Chief among those investments was a commitment to loan Clean Energy Fuels $150 million to help them build LNG refueling stations around the country in a program known as America's Natural Gas Highway®. Chesapeake also made plans to build LNG plants in several oil and gas basins where they operated, convert all 4,500 of its light-duty truck fleet over to CNG and buy self-contained CNG stations newly-developed by GE. Ironically, these steps to invest in natural gas fueling infrastructure came about at the same time Chesapeake was remaking itself over more as an oil and "liquids" producer than a natural gas company.*

The accumulating debt borne by Chesapeake, Aubrey McClendon's other problems at the helm of the company and the reduced focus on natural gas caused the company to progressively unravel these investments. By 2013, McClendon was forced out of Chesapeake, which sold its debt and small stake in Clean Energy Fuels, laid off its CNG development team and cancelled plans for further LNG development.

††††

By late 2013 Encana was also taking steps to exit the business of selling natural gas fuel products and services (but still using the fuel in its own operations). Nevertheless, Encana's and Chesapeake's efforts to use LNG and CNG

LNG supply system for oil & gas
Photo credit: Apache Corporation

were the first and second in a series of falling dominoes. Soon, other (mainly large independent oil and gas)

* Liquids refer to hydrocarbons heavier than methane but lighter than oil, like the ethane used to manufacture chemicals and propane used in barbeques and heating.

companies like Apache Corporation and Noble Energy joined and altogether created what is clearly the most important turning point in the natural gas fuels industry by kickstarting broader interest.*

Spurred by reading about Encana, Chesapeake, Apache and Noble, the C-level executives of many other top oil and gas companies began asking "Why aren't we doing this?" and pushed their operations teams to at least test LNG (or CNG) for drilling. They sometimes even created something of a public relations feeding frenzy trying to notch industry firsts. Thus, for example, the Pittsburgh-based EQT Corporation was the first to announce the use of LNG for drilling in the northeast (running the LNG in together with diesel in the so-called "dual-fuel" mode) and another company, Seneca Resources, touted that it was the first in the northeast to use LNG for drilling in 100% dedicated natural gas-fueled engines.

††††

So, the first way the oil & gas industry propelled the natural gas fuels industry forward was by proving that LNG and CNG are acceptable and cost-effective alternatives to diesel in high horsepower engines, applications where a lot of fuel could be displaced. This potential bonanza in natural gas fuel demand growth expanded interest in LNG and CNG beyond the realm of cars, buses and trucks, which was where nearly all of the focus had been since the 1990s.

Of course, how much fuel can be consumed is a function of an engine's size (measured in horsepower or volume displacement) and how much of the time it runs. In comparison with a 150–200 horsepower car that uses a few gallons of fuel a day or a 350–450 horsepower

---

* These companies and others have also used practically-raw natural gas from the producing fields and uncompressed pipeline gas. When they are available and of sufficient quality, these are fully acceptable and inexpensive fueling solutions, much like all the other pipeline gas already in wide use.

tractor-trailer that might use one hundred gallons a day, drilling requires engines that are up to over 2,000 horsepower and consume over one thousand gallons of fuel a day.

People in the industry found it exciting that drilling could use over a thousand gallons a day of natural gas fuels. But, there was even greater potential in completion operations (known throughout the industry as "hydraulic fracturing" and more popularly referred to as "fraccing") that created another level of customer excitement. Hydraulic fracturing operations use ten to twenty or more 2,000+ horsepower engines simultaneously to inject the massive amounts of water underground. This creates the potential to use up to about twenty thousand gallons a day of LNG or CNG at a single site.

A few oil and gas companies took the lead here, also. Notably, Apache Corporation quietly began testing natural gas fuels for this purpose in Alberta Canada and then subsequently expanded to Oklahoma and Texas. By 2013, Apache was able to tout that it had converted an entire hydraulic fracturing operation consisting of over 25,000 horsepower of engines to run on a combination of LNG and diesel. Other oil and gas companies followed suit and, like drilling, hydraulic fracturing began to emerge as a promising niche market of its own for natural gas fuels.

The second way oil and gas operations propelled the LNG and CNG market forward was by interesting some of the United States' largest manufacturing companies to take a closer look at the market. Chief among these was Caterpillar ("CAT"), the country's largest supplier of heavy machinery and, as previously noted, a former leader in the manufacture of diesel truck engines).

CAT happened to be the largest supplier of engines to the oil and gas well drilling and completions market. So, when small start-ups began tinkering with engines with the expectation of developing technology to convert them to natural gas fueling (generally by combining diesel and natural gas in the engine), they naturally turned to the CAT engines first as the most important addressable market. A few such companies, such as American Power Group and GTI Altronics, have been quite successful at making these conversions. Executives at CAT watched this effort and realized that *they* should be able to convert their own engines and also seed the market for a next generation of improved natural gas-fueled engines that could be used there. While they were successful in entering this market niche by 2012, the more important implication for CAT was that they now were in a position to lead the transition from diesel to natural gas in a wide range of large engines.

†††

Oil and gas well drilling and hydraulic fracturing operations were the clear catalysts for a rapid acceleration of commercial interest in LNG and CNG. But this use is intrinsically rather small compared to the much larger available market. Specifically, less than 2 billion gallons of diesel are used in drilling and hydraulic fracturing in the U.S. annually. Now, 2 billion gallons is pretty significant considering it created a multi-billion market opportunity for LNG and CNG, but it is only one percent of the total of the nearly 200 billion gallons of gasoline and diesel consumed. With the door opened a crack wider for CNG and LNG, this larger prize appeared to be more accessible.

A Few Words About Horizontal Drilling, Hydraulic Fracturing and Shale

It's long been known that shales are often the original source of oil and gas, and still tend to be full of these hydrocarbons. But, over geologic time, some of the oil and gas flowed out into more permeable sandstone and limestone rocks, where they've since remained. Because the oil and gas flows quite easily through these latter types of rocks, it's relatively easy to recover them. So that is where most oil and gas exploitation has occurred.

But, most of the original oil and gas remained trapped in the shale. Mitchell Energy, a relatively small and independent oil and gas drilling company named after founder George Mitchell, was the first company to apply a combination of novel techniques to unlock natural gas from the shale trap. Mitchell Energy experimented with drilling down to the shale and turning the drill bit and pipe sideways to target the almost-always horizontal shale, then shooting explosives through the pipe wall and into the shale to fracture it, thus artificially increasing its permeability. Then, by injecting massive amounts of sand suspended in water into the shale, they could prop it open and allow the gas to flow out to the surface. (This "hydraulic fracturing" process is sometimes called fraccing or fracking and has become highly controversial. Natural gas advocates typically use the "fraccing" spelling, while natural gas detractors almost universally use "fracking", likely because it's reminiscent of another "f" word. Aubrey McClendon has called the vocal anti-natural gas contingent, i.e., the frack-based spellers "Fractivists".)

Mitchell's company applied this horizontal drilling/ hydraulic fracturing method first in the Barnett Shale in north central Texas around Dallas. Mitchell sold the business to Devon Energy in 2002, and Devon continued to apply these methods in the Barnett and later the Marcellus shale in Pennsylvania. The methods Mitchell and Devon used were not exactly secrets; however, they were not broadcast either, as the secrecy provided a strong competitive advantage. During 2007 and the beginning of 2008, word spread more quickly about these techniques. Companies started applying them in the Fayetteville Shale in Arkansas and later the Haynesville Shale in Louisiana and elsewhere, getting results like those in the Barnett. The true impacts of shale gas took a few years to become accepted. But, eventually, gas prices dropped as more and more shale gas reserves were discovered, drilled and brought to market.

Just as the shale gas revolution started in 2008, within a few years geologists and businessmen had the logical idea that the same techniques could be applied to oil. They tested this out and found entirely new oil reserves, sometimes sitting alongside the shale gas. (Despite the large amount of shale oil being produced in North America, oil is priced based on international market forces like rapidly growing demand in China, India and elsewhere. So, its price hasn't declined the way natural gas has.)

12

"Song of a New Race"
(W. G. Still)

The emergence of natural gas fueling for drilling rigs could be compared to thoroughbred horses entering the starting gates before a race. It took some time for the horses to settle to the point where the gates could be opened.

Let's peg 2010 or 2011 as the year the gates opened. Energy professionals had a lot to digest before that. The "shale gas revolution" didn't start in earnest until 2008, when the positive impact of horizontal drilling and hydraulic fracturing on gas production trends first began to emerge out of the static of day-to-day and month-to-month fluctuations. In fact, natural gas prices rose to an all-time high during weather-induced shortages in the second half of 2008 at a time when more analytical minds might have cautioned (but generally did not) that supplies could rise and long-term trend in prices would be downward.

Few people were that prescient and the early believers in shale gas were outnumbered by those who believed it was a flash in the pan at best and a scam to separate investors from their money at worst. The long subsequent decline in gas prices after mid-2008 caused a form of cognitive dissonance: a fleet manager recommending in 2009 or even much of 2010 that the company's executive management should support a move to natural gas fuels because of a long-term price advantage would have found his position difficult to defend.

It wasn't until late in 2010 or 2011 that the two-year long drop in gas prices became ingrained in industry insiders' minds and accepted as a macro-trend. This was a true paradigm shift, a generational change affecting the enormous pipeline natural gas market that would also improve the competitiveness of America's domestic chemicals and manufacturing industries. That macro-trend all but drowned out the fact that such low feedstock prices would also significantly improve the opportunity for LNG and CNG fuels to flourish. By 2012, the smoke cleared from the track enough to enable one to see that the horses had already left the starting gate.

13

"Can-Utility and the Coastliners"
(Genesis)

lectric and gas utilities have gotten a bad rap
from much of the business world. A typical gripe
is that they operate as monopolies in their service
territories and therefore don't have to operate with the
usual eye towards cost management and profitability.
They're also often viewed as overly cautious and risk-averse.
While there is arguably some truth to these views, the easy
counter-argument is that utilities provide an important
service for most of the U.S. population and have offered
some of the best, most predictable returns for investors
for decades. Utilities now also offer some of the best and
brightest prospects for success in the natural gas fuels area.

Of course, the natural gas utilities deserve some of the
credit for having helped to bootstrap the nascent CNG
fueling industry back in the 1990s, but their efforts until
recently had a relatively minor impact. This has changed
as the attractiveness of the natural gas fuels industry has
increased, and it has been fully enabled by regulatory
changes enacted in 2005 that affect utilities' charters,
enabling them to split into different businesses that coexist
under parent holding companies.

Utilities have been highly regulated by state boards
and commissions. When they've split out entrepreneurial
business entities, these are referred to as 'unregulated
subsidiaries' while the relict traditional businesses are
called 'regulated subsidiaries'. Unregulated subsidiaries
operate under different rules than traditional regulated
utility companies. In effect, they are simply much like
any private company, trying to grow while keeping an
eye on risk and return. They can't rely on the regulated
businesses' ratepayers to subsidize their investments.

They do, however, benefit in other ways, like having a deep, embedded understanding of their product (natural gas), access to knowledge of pipeline regulations and in the case of LNG having access to the LNG peak shaving plants invested in long ago by their regulated subsidiary brethren.* Let's look at three important recent examples of utility activities in natural gas fuels that represent the broader potential.

†††

Atlanta Gas Light, now known at the parent company level as AGL Resources, has a history extending back to before the Civil War. In fact, the fire started by Union troops at its Atlanta gas works in 1864 was immortalized in the climactic scene of the movie "Gone with the Wind". The company trades on the stock market under the amusing symbol "GAS". It provides service as a typical natural gas utility in such disparate places as through-out the southeast, Illinois, Virginia, Maryland and New Jersey, and has other operations in Texas, Louisiana and California. But, its headquarters and heart are in Georgia and AGL has entered both the CNG and LNG businesses from this base.

AGL's CNG business has grown from its regulated subsidiary, which received approval from the Georgia Public Service Commission in 2011 to build and own CNG stations so long as it didn't increase costs for AGL's core rate paying customers. AGL's plans were opposed by some who feared the competition, but AGL prevailed and began building stations in 2012.

Atlanta is an excellent jumping off point for AGL's CNG business. It's at the confluence of interstate highways that

* There is often a very thick wall between the regulated and unregulated subsidiaries in order to avoid granting the utilities unfair competitive advantages. In some cases, an outsider can talk to people in both sides of the utility's business, but the two sides of the business can't always talk to each other.

connect the area to all major population centers along the east and Gulf coasts and Midwest, and is itself a densely populated metropolitan area. This situation provides an even better set of dynamics for LNG.

AGL's utility business is blessed with ownership of four legacy LNG peak shaving plants stretching from Chattanooga, Tennessee to central Georgia. These plants are now being pressed into service by the unregulated side of the business for use in natural gas fueling. AGL established a subsidiary, Pivotal LNG, which has started to develop the merchant LNG business serving heavy-duty trucks owned by companies like UPS, and the oil and gas industry (including, as previously noted, Encana).

More recently, Pivotal has leveraged its ownership of the LNG in the peak-shaving plant tanks to win the opportunity to supply LNG to marine vessels in Jacksonville, Florida. This is a strikingly important development; many companies lined up to bid to supply this early adopter of LNG for marine fueling, TOTE, from new plants located right in Jacksonville, but Pivotal was the only company that had sufficient LNG already available close enough to Jacksonville to be able to truck product to meet TOTE's dockside needs while also preparing to build a plant close by.*

The broader importance of Pivotal's win is that it indicates to all of the other peak-shaving LNG plant owners that their incumbent ownership of these plants can provide a strong competitive advantage in the business. It's even more striking given the fact that AGL would not consider diverting any of its LNG from the peak-shaving plants in order to serve the merchant LNG business as little as ten years ago.

†††

AGL set the standard and showed the way, but numerous other utilities have closely followed. Among these, the

---

* Pivotal established a joint venture with a firm new to the LNG business, Wespac, to build this new plant.

Reading, Pennsylvania-based natural gas utility, UGI Corporation, has also leveraged its LNG peak shaver for the LNG market. Interestingly, UGI's efforts in this area were led by John Walsh, who previously had worked at the industrial gas company BOC, so he was well-versed in cryogenic product businesses. UGI also owns Amerigas, which is a major supplier of propane, so the company has familiarity with the fuels industry and that factor has also helped them make the leap into LNG.

In developing the business, UGI was not able to get unencumbered access to the fuel from UGI's LNG liquefier or adjacent peak-shaving storage tank due to the kind of utility regulatory restraints mentioned above. So they took the extraordinary step of spending nearly $100 million to build a completely new LNG storage tank and truck loading facility next to the existing peak-shaving plant's tank, an amount of money that is possibly more than UGI would have spent to build a completely new LNG production plant and (smaller) storage tank.

†††

Let's turn our attention to a utility that has had more involvement in CNG, but has the opportunity to leverage LNG assets as well, the holding company Integrys Energy Group.

Recall that by 2011 Cy Wagner and Jack Brown were reaching ages where they felt it best to divest their Pinnacle and Trillium CNG businesses. Integrys bought both of these businesses with plans to diversify them more and more into the public fueling station space and lower their reliance on the bread-and-butter transit bus business. For instance, Integrys management worked on building up a joint venture to help dairy cooperatives move milk products with CNG fuel, while another JV called EVO Trillium was set up with a Freightliner dealer in Arizona to shift local customers of Freightliner trucks to CNG. EVO

Trillium has grown to a national scale serving some large common carrier fleets like Swift and Central Freight.

Integrys now operates all of its CNG business under the Trillium brand and is on course to have one hundred stations soon and likely to have built three hundred stations by the year 2020, potentially maintaining them in second place behind Clean Energy Fuels in the CNG business.* (Note: An announcement was made in July 2014 that Integrys was to be bought by another utility, Wisconsin Energy Corp.)

†††

Other utilities are also pressing into the CNG market and the trend will expand. For example, the utility behind the original development of Utah's CNG infrastructure, Questar, is expanding its footprint nationwide and is poised to be a major factor in the industry.

Like AGL in Georgia, NW Natural in Oregon applied to its state regulatory commission for permission to build and own CNG stations there. And like the AGL proposal, this was fought by competitors in the natural gas fuels business on the basis that NW Natural could gain from an uneven playing field. However, the commission sided with the utility on the grounds that none of the other companies had pursued any sort of CNG station build-out in Oregon and that the state wanted to encourage this any way they could. The larger takeaway is that the utility companies are here to stay in the CNG markets.

Similarly, other utilities are following AGL's and UGI's lead into the LNG market. These include the Indianapolis utility Citizen's Energy (through a new subsidiary, Kinetrix), Philadelphia-based PECO and Memphis Gas Light & Water. Undoubtedly, more will follow.

---

* In comparison, Clean Energy already has business at five hundred stations.

14

"Blue Days"
(Buddy Holly)

I t's become extremely popular to use a shortened version of the word 'blue' to brand something distinctive. Johnson Barnes is a rapper and hip hop artist born in 1983 in Los Angeles who goes by the name Blu. An Italian-born artist who chooses to keep his identity hidden also uses that name. It's also the brand name of an e-cigarette that glows blue instead of the usual red-flame color of normal cigarettes. Natural gas typically burns with a blue flame so that color is used in virtually all of the natural gas industry's advertising and promotion.* So, it's not surprising that Blu was also selected to brand a new, upstart company.

Blu LNG is the brainchild of an entrepreneur from northern Utah, Merritt Norton. Merritt grew up in a Mormon family and his father ran a trucking fleet. It's convenient to conclude that trucking ran in Merritt's blood and he was, in fact, drawn to the business, yet he has taken an untraditional trajectory during his career.

Merritt worked for some time at Cummins, the manufacturer that has practically cornered the natural gas fuels truck engine market (as well as having the largest share of the diesel truck engine market) in the U.S. He also spent time working for Prometheus Energy, the company re-formed after the demise of CryoFuel Systems that initially worked on building renewable LNG projects. He left Prometheus during a company downturn determined to start up his own LNG fuel supply and technology company.

---

* In addition, the mega-retailer of propane, Blue Rhino, evokes that fuel's blue flame color as well.

He relocated from Washington State to Provo, Utah and set up what was essentially a one-man shop called CH_4 Energy.* Using his own money plus angel investor funds, he started demonstrating how to convert existing diesel trucks to natural gas fuels working with the local Cummins dealership and actually worked out of their garage. Simultaneously, he leveraged contacts at Flying J, one of the largest companies in North America in the truck stop business, engaging executives there in the possibility of co-locating LNG refueling systems along-side diesel to serve what Merritt was confident would be a significant and fairly rapid switch to LNG. The concept is reminiscent of Clean Energy Fuels' America's Natural Gas Highway program, but in fact CH4's conceptualization of this approach may have predated Clean Energy's implementation of it by a few years. Flying J personnel were quite intrigued with the idea and saw it as a means to grow in what was otherwise a business that sees flat-lining revenues.

Then, financial catastrophe hit Flying J from an oil deal gone awry. The company invested in the Longhorn oil pipeline, which traveled through El Paso, Texas. When petroleum prices were gyrating wildly in 2008, Flying J had the pipeline full of crude oil acquired at over $140 per barrel. But when the pipeline had to temporarily shut down and prices simultaneously fell through the floor, the company was stuck with millions of barrels now worth, at best, only $100 per barrel. The company was in bankruptcy almost immediately, effectively killing the chances to cooperate with CH_4.

The sole investment made by Merritt with Flying J was the installation of his first LNG station, now branded with the "Blu" label, adjacent to Flying J's truck stop in South Salt Lake. Meantime, Flying J sold all of its U.S. stations to its largest competitor, Pilot, who soon after partnered with Clean Energy on development of America's Natural Gas Highway.

* CH_4 is the chemical formula for methane.

This first Blu station was paid for by Merritt along with his angel investors. He used the station as a flagship to attract local truck fleets to consider using LNG (and CNG made from the LNG right at the station), as well as to showcase the new natural gas fuels business model for other potential investors. In a bit of irony, Blu hired a Wyoming-based LNG station supplier NorthStar, Inc. to begin building the South Salt Lake station in mid 2010,

Blu LNG's South Salt Lake station
Photo credit: Blu LNG

but before the end of 2010, NorthStar was acquired by Clean Energy Fuels. So, in effect, Blu lost both its prospective truck stop partner and its station supplier to its largest competitor in the LNG business.

In a stroke of luck, Merritt attended the natural gas fuels industry trade group's annual meeting in Dallas in 2011 where he met a potential investor from the Chinese company ENN. Roaming around the meeting during a break he ran into Jun Yung, who was an executive at ENN responsible for their building hundreds of CNG and LNG stations in China. When Merritt inquired what Jun – who barely spoke English – was doing there, Jun replied he was looking for possible investments in natural gas fuels in the U.S. Since Merritt was there looking for potential investors, the two began talking and within a year ENN had acquired fifty percent of Blu's business, creating the company now named Transfuels.

Transfuels announced plans to build five hundred stations across the U.S., including fifty in 2013 alone, as well as LNG plants to supply them. Transfuels also bought trucks to loan out to prospective customers in order to try using LNG before committing to big-time change-overs of their fleets. ENN was pushing money at Transfuels to try and gain a jump on Clean Energy by building more stations faster.

The company's appetite for speed, however, began to outrun the trucking industry's adoption of natural gas fuels. By the end of 2013 Transfuels had scaled back its plans, anticipating building only a total of two dozen or so stations before making further commitments. In addition, Jun was both out of ENN and no longer involved in Transfuels, removed by his superiors in China. Transfuels laid off twenty percent of the 200 employees it had hired since forming the company in early 2012.

Transfuels continues to operate in this slightly reduced mode and is likely well poised to accelerate its activities again as the market advances.

15

"Hey Hey"
(Big Bill Broonzy)

Still looking to develop new LNG projects in 2007, Ken Kelley approached some of his business associates to explore the opportunity of building an LNG plant for the ripening natural gas fuels market in Peru. Among the people he spoke to was George Yates, one of the largest producers of oil in New Mexico who had inherited his father Harvey E. Yates' company, HEYCO Energy. Ken convinced George and another investor, Willy Neustadtl, to join him in this project, which they dubbed Irradia. George took a twenty percent share and Willy and Ken each took forty percent.

Unfortunately, the global economic crisis followed soon after and Irradia lost their financing. George took his other two partners out and went from a minority interest to owning the plant, even though he had no immediate plans for it. The plant parts were scattered – some in the plant builder's (Salof) yard, pieces in Louisiana, some in Peru and some that still hadn't shipped from the sub-system manufacturers.

In 2011, George met with Aubrey McClendon, who was still running Chesapeake. Aubrey asked him if he realized what was going on with shale gas pushing the potential for LNG in the U.S. After more discussions, Aubrey convinced George to erect the plant here. George hired Chris Coleman, who had been helping Trillium and a private equity group, and understood the mechanics of capital raises that could help develop the plant into a new business.

The original thought was to put the plant in the middle of the Texas Triangle where it would be local to the expectant truck fleet market. George and Chris then started looking at the pro-forma and realized that drilling and hydraulic fracturing was the short-term opportunity to build the business around and that transportation was the long-term play. They also realized that nobody else was stepping up to the plate to build new LNG plants in Texas despite numerous rumors. HEYCO understood they had an inside track on the market: they possessed the building blocks of the sizable (120,000-plus gallon per day) plant that George had bought and further calculated that the plant capacity could be doubled for not a lot of additional capital.

In 2012, HEYCO was still focused on southern Texas but nothing was happening. Salof began pressuring HEYCO to get the plant out of their yard because its business was now churning faster due partly to new plant orders from Shell (see next chapter). Finally by late 2013, HEYCO struck two critical deals. In the first, they acquired land adjacent to a natural gas processing plant where good gas quality and volumes could be assured. Second, a subsidiary of a 150-year old Japanese company, Itochu, agreed to take the product and distribute it in the region.

In sum, HEYCO is a promising upstart in the LNG business, although it remains to be seen how successfully their plant will compete with other companies whose plans in the region have also begun gelling.

16

"Shell Shock"
(Heart)

Royal Dutch Shell is one of the largest corporations in the world, reaching $450 billion in revenues during 2013. Shell is best known for its petroleum business, but the company is also the largest producer and trader of LNG, which it does on the international market, producing LNG at scales much larger than needed for the natural gas fuels market and shipping it in trans-oceanic tankers.

With this background in large-scale LNG, Shell entered the market for LNG at a scale useful for natural gas fuels in Scandinavia with the acquisition of Gasnor, a specialist in that business, and in North America. The North American efforts were launched only a few years ago and have thus far followed an arc-like trajectory of attempted dominance in 2012–2013 followed by a near-complete pullback in 2014, leaving Shell's LNG plans largely in limbo. Let's examine this more closely.

Throughout the past half century, Shell has been an innovator in both core and peripheral business areas. A good example is the company's decades-long effort to find economic ways to convert natural gas to diesel-like products via a set of processes referred to generically as gas-to-liquids (or GTL). After many years, dollars and man-hours of research and development, Shell built a refinery-scale GTL plant in Qatar. When first planned, the cost of this plant was expected to be $5 billion but it wound up costing between $19 and $24 billion (reported costs vary). Shell also planned to build another $20 billion GTL plant in Louisiana owing to the same low-cost natural gas environment in North America that has also encouraged opportunities in the natural gas fuels industry. This GTL plant was cancelled by Shell late in 2013 along with other pullbacks in planned investments.

By contrast with the time and money poured into GTL, it seemed reasonable that Shell would also engage in the small-scale LNG fuels industry because the plants would cost "only" hundreds of millions of dollars each. Shell did engage, forming a team in Houston that assessed the opportunity and announced plans to build plants in Louisiana, Alberta and Ontario, plus another location yet to be selected. They then commissioned Salof – prior to Salof's acquisition by GE (see Chapter 18) – to build the plants. The Louisiana location could serve marine vessels converting to LNG in the Gulf Coast and Mississippi River and the Ontario plant was planned for the city of Sarnia near the banks of Lake Huron. Shell logically planned to base-load these plants with customers in the marine LNG market (Chapter 28).

Somewhat surprisingly, Shell's plans were to build relatively large "small-scale" plants, each of which could produce 240,000 gallons of LNG per day and easily be doubled in size; this compares with all of the existing merchant LNG plants to date, none of which is larger and only one of which approaches this size. It was a bold move: Shell's logic was that they could sign marine shipping companies to consume a significant amount of this production and then also generate sales with truck fleets and other markets extending for large distances around these plants. Perhaps even more surprising, according to Shell the Alberta plant was dependent mainly on the heavy-duty trucking market along the Trans-Canada Highway and between Edmonton and Calgary. Such a plant would require something like two million trucks to sop up all the product the plant could produce, which was far larger than the local addressable market.

Shell viewed these LNG plants as similar to their refineries, from which they serve regional markets for trucks, ships and other fuel consumers with petroleum products. In promoting the LNG plants, Shell touted that their experience in global-scale LNG created a unique set of capabilities unmatchable by its smaller competitors. But, in the end, Shell found that sales volumes from committed customers didn't provide the security needed to follow through on its plans. In pulling back, it appears that Shell may have actually fallen back into its comfort zone, repurposing the liquefaction plants already under construction for use in a global-scale LNG export terminal at Elba Island, Georgia that Shell partly owns.

Shell's decision to slow its investments in LNG fuels can also be attributed to a new CEO at the company who has strongly advocated "disciplined capital investment" since taking over. Along with the plants, Shell also scaled back its plans to build LNG fueling stations across Canada and the U.S. from an expected 100 stations down to just 20. To date, only a few stations have been built, including one near the defunct Alberta plant and one in southern California to serve the trucking firm CR England.

Shell says it stands by its commitments to supply customers that had been relying on these plants and also states that its decision to pull back from the LNG natural gas fuels market is not a decision to pull out, but rather that the company will follow through when the time is right.

17

"The Caterpillar Crawl"
(The Moffatts)

It was noted earlier that Caterpillar was sidelined from the U.S. on-highway truck engine market in the 2000s and that the company watched as several engine technology start-ups began to convert CAT's market-dominating engines to natural gas for the oil and gas market. Working with remarkable speed for a large, multi-centralized organization, CAT executives jumped in and decided that CAT would, without question, be a major player in the natural gas-fueled equipment business.

At a trade conference in September 2012 attended by over a thousand industry officials, CAT's head of the business announced that the company was "all-in" pursuing both natural gas-fueled engines and the equipment they're used in. This signaled an intent to lead the development of technology for LNG and CNG in ships, locomotives, and drilling and hydraulic fracturing, as well as for heavy-duty mining equipment – a key market overall for CAT and a niche opportunity for natural gas fuels that may grow to a significant scale within a few years.

In many markets like heavy-duty engines for stationary power generation, ships and trains, as well as some equipment the engines are dropped into, CAT's main competitor is GE. In particular, the two firms go head-to-head as the only significant suppliers of locomotives in the country. Both see the potential for strong adoption of LNG to fuel railroads and are very actively attempting to gain a leadership position. It should be exciting to watch this rivalry develop. In the next chapter, we'll explore GE's assault on the natural gas fuels market in more detail.

18

"The General Electric"
(Shihad)

Perhaps no company exemplifies the progress made in the past few years and the future promise of natural gas fuels better than GE. While the entrances of other large multi-nationals like Caterpillar and Shell were significant, GE is the largest brick-and-mortar company in the U.S. and one of the largest in the world. It has taken a large, diverse position in LNG and CNG as a supplier of fueling equipment and production plants and has also spiced its position in typical GE fashion by providing financing to customers for these goods.

In the broadest context, GE tends to develop large, diverse positions in large attractive business "platforms", which create a foundation around which they can focus on a customer segment and inter-related sets of needs. Then, GE invests in these platforms via acquisitions, R&D and technology partnerships.

GE has recognized the transition from petroleum to natural gas and from conventional to unconventional (shale) oil and gas, as well as the increasingly complex role of technology to extract and transport them. So, unsurprisingly, GE developed a platform around this industry.

GE is extremely adept at squeezing costs out of their products; I doubt that any mega-company is better than GE at taking this approach. An earlier example of GE's approach to business that is related to the natural gas industry occurred in the 1990s when GE worked intensively to improve the performance and reduce the costs of combustion turbines used to burn natural gas and produce electricity. Prior to this, natural gas-fired combustion turbines were most often used to produce spurts of power during peak demand periods, while coal boilers were used day and hour in and day and hour out.

The company adapted technologies that had been used to increase the reliability of jet aircraft engines. Just as importantly, they were able to scale these turbines up from sizes only suitable for peak demand service, when the turbines supplemented coal electric power plants, up to sizes that could actually replace those coal plants. Plus they figured out what was needed to reduce the time after an equipment breakdown to fix that equipment and get it back on-line, a process they referred to as reducing "wing-to-wing" time (a term derived from the aerospace industry).

By the end of the 1990s, GE was so successful (along with competitors that were spurred by GE) that there was a massive shift to large natural gas plants operating 24-7. The flood of new natural gas power plants was so great that the increased demand for natural gas actually pushed its price up significantly.

Another tactic that GE is good at is hiring people in straight from schools and grooming them in a very well-regimented GE mold, then advancing stars up in the organization (or, for laggards, jettisoning them from the company). The new head of GE's Oil and Gas Division, Lorenzo Simonelli, fits that mold having been born in Italy, schooled in Wales and working for the company for twenty years, advancing through the ranks before becoming the youngest division head in the organization. Speculation has been that he is being groomed to run the whole company one day and that has the possible ring of truth since his division is central to GE's entire growth strategy.

Recall that the head of Caterpillar's natural gas development business told a conference audience in 2012 that the company was "all in" with products for natural gas fuels. Simonelli made almost exactly the identical point on behalf of GE at the same trade show in 2013. GE's efforts during that year certainly suggested that was true.

Building off a deep capability in compressors that the company built from the ground up and with acquisitions, GE started down a few related paths in the natural gas fueling space. First, and obviously, GE was able to apply its skills to build compression systems for CNG. GE's effort here has focused partly on packaging one of its compressors in a portable box known as an ISO container along with a gas dryer to remove water, a fuel dispenser and a system controller. Being essentially a system in a box that could be easily hooked up to a feeder gas pipeline – for plug-and-play natural gas in, CNG out – GE creatively named it CNG in a Box™. Chesapeake's Peake Fuel Solutions group collaborated with GE on the development and to deliver its first deployment in 2012. But even after Chesapeake ran into the problems described in Chapter 11 and left the natural gas fuels business, GE continued to advance CNG in a Box.

Maintaining this high level of naming creativity, GE also developed an LNG in a Box™ system, which it introduced in 2013. While also plug-and-play, this system is considerably more complicated than the comparable one for CNG. Basically, it is a scaled-down, fully complete LNG production plant, plus a storage tank and an LNG fueling system. It is considerably more expensive than the CNG system, but its performance makes it suitable for truck fleets that need enough LNG fuel for up to 50–100 trucks and want to make the LNG right on-site (as opposed to trucking it in from a plant somewhere else). GE was able to sell a handful of systems to a European company, Gasfin, and has been looking for customers here in the U.S.

LNG in a Box is a neat self-contained solution, but being so small it is often at a cost disadvantage compared with the 'truck it in and dispense it' LNG supply solution. Recognizing this, GE also made some bold moves in developing, building and selling larger scale LNG plants. Chief among these was its acquisition of the Salof Corporation, a 200-employee Texas-based builder of LNG (and CO_2) plants, named after its founder George Salof. Salof had had some success selling LNG plants overseas, but its success in the U.S. was limited. They did, however, make progress by being selected by Shell for that company's first LNG plants destined for the North American market. In addition, Salof is on the verge of having the plant now owned by HEYCO put into service in Texas.

Just like the CNG in a Box design is able to package GE's compressors into a higher-value product, compressors are a core part of LNG plants. So, here too, GE's strategy is to move down the value chain so as to be able to get the profits from both its core technology and the full solution.

19

"We'll Sweep Out the Ashes in the Morning"
(Gram Parsons)

I t's not uncommon for large, well-established companies that should succeed in a business area to fail at being competitive with more nimble start-ups or sustainably participating in a business. Chesapeake Energy is one example of a company that had the right ingredients to succeed in natural gas fuels – strong capitalization, a visionary leader, and a high degree of motivation to succeed – but was unable to stay in the business when these ingredients collapsed.

When Chesapeake's CNG and nascent LNG businesses collapsed and the business managers were let go, it created the opportunity to remix these raw ingredients into other potential industry-leading businesses.

For example, one of the former heads of Chesapeake's CNG vehicle effort, Norman Herrera, felt the entrepreneurial bug after being let go from Chesapeake in September 2013 and created a business, Sparq Natural Gas, LLC, with two other former Chesapeake employees, Sufyan Qarni as COO and Tristan Adler as CFO. Sparq's mission is to build, own and operate CNG fueling stations at convenience stores.

Another ex-Chesapeake manager, Sarie Joubert, joined a CNG station developer, TruStar. Yet another, Scott Minton, went to OnCue Express to manage the CNG fueling business there.

TruStar, OnCue and Sparq all have the potential to be leaders in the natural gas fuels space. So the dispersal of Chesapeake's ex employees to these companies highlights the importance of "creative destruction" in allowing the sustainability of an industry in spite of the exit of any particular company.

20

"Cold Cold Cold"
(Little Feat)

C hart Industries is a billion dollar supplier of equipment focused on technologies that cool gases down to extremely low "cryogenic" temperatures. The company was launched by two brothers, Charles and Arthur Holmes, from whose first names the name Chart was created. Among its earliest product lines were systems used by sperm banks for freezing.

The company has since developed a much more diversified position in systems used to chill atmospheric gases to cryogenic temperatures (making liquid nitrogen, liquid oxygen and the like). Equipment for liquefied natural gas was also part of the company's portfolio and they became a major player in the then-small, but promising, field of LNG fueling stations during the 1990s, mainly by acquiring the major player, MVE. By the mid 2000s, stagnation in the industry caused the company to effectively shut down its LNG fueling business, although it remained active in related LNG production equipment.

When it became obvious around 2010 that the LNG industry was entering an upswing, Chart reorganized and re-entered the LNG fueling business. They re-gained a preeminent position and have been able to cite some key accomplishments, such as supplying all of the tanks for Clean Energy Fuels' build-out of stations for America's Natural Gas Highway. Chart has also been deeply involved in the Chinese market, supplying storage tanks for the market there for the past few years.

Success breeds competition and that certainly holds true here. A prime example is the firm Taylor-Wharton, a diversified company that can trace its history back to the 1700s, where it manufactured cannon balls for George Washington's Continental Army. Taylor-Wharton also has a 50+ year history in equipment useful for cryogenic applications, including large LNG tanks for fueling station storage; they also took a stab at supplying side-mounted tanks for trucks some time ago but quality problems sidelined them.

In just the past few years, seeing the trend and seeing Chart run away with much of the business, Taylor-Wharton took steps to become a leader in LNG. They lured top execs from Chart, including Eric Rottier, who had been COO for Chart's Asia business and was reportedly rebuffed from holding Chart's overall top position, as well as some of Chart's leading sales and technical people.

At present, Chart, Taylor-Wharton, another firm Indian-owned InoxCVA, and others, including Westport Innovations (see next chapter), now vie for leadership supplying the equipment needed to build LNG infra-structure, creating a healthy competitive environment.

We can expect new entrants as the market becomes more and more attractive, including companies not quite sure of the industry's future or their right to play, but still fearing the prospect they will be left behind by a swelling wave. Just recently, Lockheed Martin leveraged cryogenic fuel tank experience gained during its supply of liquid fuel tanks for NASA's space shuttle program by entering the LNG fuel tank market, initially supplying large 67,000 gallon tanks for Harvey Gulf's natural gas-fueled ships. These LNG tanks are even manufactured at the same plant in New Orleans that Lockheed Martin used for NASA.

21

"Wing and Prayer"
(The Bee Gees)

Westport Innovations is a Canadian-based firm that began in the mid 1990s focused on commercializing technology to inject natural gas at high pressures into compression ignited (diesel) engines. This approach allows LNG to displace roughly 95% of the diesel in those engines.* Early in its life, Westport also developed relationships with Cummins and is now the premier supplier of natural gas engines for heavy-duty trucks, supplying the latter's spark-ignited 100 percent natural gas-fueled engines through the Cummins Westport JV.

Westport also worked with Ford to develop engines for its F and E Series trucks and has since also teamed with Ford to consolidate all of its dedicated natural gas and bi-fuel (natural gas and gasoline) light-duty products, under a single line called the WiNG™ Power System. WiNG products include a product line acquired in a deal in which the company bought Clean Energy Fuels' "BAF" business.

Westport has been fortunate to be in a position to partner with such a diverse set of business partners, but it has also been fortunate that the Canadian Federal Government and province of British Columbia research agencies (i.e., Canada's National Research Council and the Science Council of British Columbia) have also provided a significant share of the hundreds of millions of dollars to support its R&D programs.

Along the way, the Cummins Westport 50:50 joint venture was formed in 2001 and this platform became

---

* CNG can't be used because, while it's compressed, it's not compressed to even higher pressures needed at the engine inlet.

the marketing and sales arm for Cummins-designed and built spark-ignited dedicated natural gas engines. This has proven critical to Westport, since sales of these products (in 6 and 9 liter engine sizes) for installation in medium-duty trucks and buses, and "lighter" heavy-duty trucks (again using the 9 liter engine, as well as a 12 liter size product) has generated most of the sales revenue that has helped to fund other development programs. Those development programs have proven costly: the company has built up retained losses of over $600 million.

The 12-liter, 400 horsepower Cummins Westport engine is currently considered the single greatest game changer for natural gas-fueled heavy duty trucks. After several delays in order to prove reliability and to ensure it could hold up to hard on-highway use, it was introduced commercially in 2013. It's safe to say that sufficient growth in sales of this engine will be critical for Westport's sustainable existence, as well as for the success of on-highway natural gas fuel development programs in general.

Westport's ultimate role with Cummins is not set in stone – for instance, Cummins has decided to develop and commercialize a 15-liter analogue of the 12-liter engine for the heaviest of heavy-duty tractor-trailer trucks in a few years without using the Cummins Westport JV as the channel to market. Also creating a problem for Westport, albeit a temporary one, is that in early 2014 they had to recall twenty five thousand vehicles because an engine sensor could ice up.

Meanwhile, Westport has all but dropped current development of the compression-ignited (i.e., the high pressure direct injection, or HPDI) engine for heavy-duty trucks, keeping a hand in it only with Volvo. That magnifies Westport's dependence on the spark-ignited natural gas engines.

Adapting to this situation, Westport has begun focusing on the development of HPDI engines for high horsepower applications, the type used in drilling rigs, hydraulic fracturing pumps, mining equipment, ships and locomotives. Westport has again taken the teaming approach, for example working with Caterpillar in some of these efforts.

In sum, Westport has been quite adaptive to changes in market conditions and technological needs, although they've paid a high price undertaking costly, long-term technology development efforts. Ideally, Westport will be able to continue to grow its sales of spark-ignited natural gas engines while it drives the compression-ignited engine technology and other endeavors forward, especially in the emerging high horsepower applications. At the same time, it appears that Cummins will be the company to beat in the market for the 15-liter engine tractor-trailer truck market.

22

"Downsize Blues"

(Dick Siegel)

N ew industries, products and businesses inevitably encounter rough stretches, so participants and followers have to be ready for roller coaster-like ups and downs with regard to expectations and results. The natural gas fuels industry is not immune from this.

In 2012 and through at least the first half of 2013, there was a high degree of optimism. After all, there was much anticipation that the Cummins Westport 12-liter 400 horsepower engine would allow the on-highway truck market to break wide open. This was matched by statements from customers like FritoLay, UPS and Proctor & Gamble that CNG and LNG were fuels of choice. CAT and subsequently GE said they were "all in" with products for natural gas fuels, including supplying engines and locomotive tender cars, while four major railroads were at least experimenting with LNG. GE had just invested in Salof's LNG plant capability, boats were beginning to convert and there were new entrants like Stabilis and HEYCO ready to invest in plants to serve the Texas LNG market. The future never looked brighter.

Thus, it was something of a shock when some of the leading guard and fast industry followers stumbled during late 2013 and into 2014. First, Clean Energy Fuels was the subject of several critical articles in the on-line investment press. In October 2013 Piper Jaffrey lowered its expectations for Clean Energy's stock price, predicting a drop from around $12 at the time to $4.50, whereas previously it had predicted a bottom of $9.50.* The lowered guidance was based on predictions of slower growth for LNG versus CNG in trucks, which was expected to work against Clean Energy's recent investment bias toward LNG stations and plans for LNG plant investments.

Clean Energy fought back with pointed comments aimed at defusing Piper Jaffrey's arguments, including countering that the company was also heavily invested in CNG stations and that CNG still accounts for the majority of the company's revenues. However, Clean Energy added fuel to the fire with announcements that were perceived by some to include questionable data and fuzzy math. For example, it announced that its customers had ordered 70% more natural gas vehicles in the first three quarters of 2013 compared with the same period in 2012. This statement could have been interpreted to mean that Clean Energy's sales were increasing at a similar pace, but it ignored that many customers – for instance UPS – were also buying natural gas fuels from Clean Energy's competitors. So, it was nice information to have about the overall market trend but many people felt that it didn't necessarily reflect immediate dividends for Clean Energy's business.

Things turned even worse for Clean Energy in 2014 as the company was hit by more negative press, resulting in the stock dropping in one day, on February 5th, from $11.50 to below $10.00. Disappointing 2013 end-of-year earnings and lack of guidance in future results caused another huge drop on February 28th to the low $8.00s per share. (As explained more completely in the Afterword, a start-up business is like a roller coaster and Clean Energy Fuels' stock and business prospects may rise as quickly as they fall.)

---

* Before this, Clean Energy's stock had been range-bound to a large extent, bouncing between about $12–14 per share since mid-2012. Good for short-term traders, but bad for stock buy-and-hold investors. The analyst reports caused a quick drop from the high $13.00s to the low $11.00s.

While Clean Energy had tried to promote the edges of its core business by touting its renewable natural gas fuels efforts and plans to build LNG plants with GE and Ferus, the root cause of the problems was that the core on-highway market's adoption rate was slower than expected, causing openings of the LNG stations to be delayed. Many stations were completed, but not opened for business.

Clean Energy wasn't the only company to see lowered expectations for highway LNG fueling. Transfuels (Blu LNG) announced in February 2014 that it was cutting back the pace of development until the market dictated it act more aggressively and laid off 20% of its staff (which had grown from a few people to over 200 people in just two years). At the helm of Transfuels, Merritt Norton reported that he expected LNG-fueled trucks would take off once the cost differential versus diesel trucks came down. Merritt's prediction was that the current $40,000–80,000 difference in the cost of trucks would decline to zero difference within three years.

Shell, the slowest to actually invest in LNG stations, also cut back its plans in early 2014. Only one fueling station was completed (in Alberta, Canada), one more was planned (in southern California) and plans for further growth were called into question. As noted before, Shell also retracted its plans to build LNG plants in Alberta, Ontario and Louisiana.

Somewhat disturbingly, Encana, the company that was responsible for jump-starting growth in the natural gas fuels industry a few years earlier by converting drilling rigs over, encouraging Heckmann to convert its trucks to LNG and building fueling stations, decided to call it quits, putting its natural gas fuels business up for sale. Encana's actions were not totally unexpected because, just like it's competitor, Chesapeake Energy (and also Shell), Encana felt that cutting out non-core, non-essential businesses was critical in order to bring the company back to financial health.

The specific causes of the pullbacks and the lessons learned by Clean Energy, Transfuels, Shell and Encana are each unique. But, they reinforce the fact that in developing a new industry some companies can be successfully committed for the long haul, but many others will stumble, awaiting others willing to pick up the pieces when this happens. This dynamic will inevitably extend into the future.

23

"Don't Worry About the Government"
(Talking Heads)

B efore turning to the course of the business today, it's worth backing up and looking at how the government has also influenced the natural gas fuels industry.

Recall that the Federal government's 1992 EPACT law propelled interest in natural gas fuels by forcing government fleets to buy dual-fuel vehicles, thus encouraging natural gas utilities to erect CNG stations, but that effort fizzled out. For some, that is evidence enough that the government should simply let market forces take over. However, the Federal and many state governments have stayed involved and the interplay between business interests and policy makers is certainly worth a look.

†††

The natural gas industry has long been a poor cousin to the petroleum industry at the national level. Large multinational oil companies have had money, lobbying power and influence in Washington that the mainly-independent natural gas producers haven't. Compounding this is the fact that natural gas producers, pipeline companies and gas utilities have often acted independently, setting up different industry trade groups that barely interacted for many years. Additionally, the natural gas fuels industry's trade group, NGVAmerica, has been small in comparison with other organizations, with an annual budget of only about $1 million. NGVAmerica's influence pales in comparison to, say, the ethanol fuel industry's Renewable Fuels Association and the smaller, more grass-rootsy American Coalition for Ethanol, which both have the backing of farm interests since ethanol comes predominantly from corn.

NGVAmerica has boot-strapped the effort to create and sustain incentives for natural gas fuels, sometimes being able to ride the coattails of other alternative fuels and sometimes working at odds with them when their interests diverged. Helpfully, they've been able to secure substantial Federal incentives for CNG and LNG, but in recent years those incentives have been extended only from one year to the next. Of course, any potential new customer is not going to factor in the benefits of these incentives for the life of a vehicle when it can't be counted on for more than a year.

T. Boone Pickens, the billionaire founder of Clean Energy Fuels, has been NGVAmerica's steadfast accomplice in advocating for natural gas fuels.* Pickens has made a virtual career of talking up these fuels with government officials and in the public media, sometimes through business networks like CNBC. He established "The Pickens Plan", which promotes the use of natural gas fuels as the centerpiece of a program that reduces our dependence on foreign oil. At the same time, he has tried to get the Federal government to strengthen and lengthen the incentives for CNG and LNG, as well as natural gas vehicles and fueling stations. (Of course, these incentives benefit Clean Energy Fuels, so public opinion is somewhat divided on whether the Pickens Plan is driven by Boone's patriotism and true concern over oil imports or his interest in protecting his investment. It's probably a combination.)

Pickens has cozied up to and been embraced by Democrats as much as Republicans, and perhaps even more so due to the former's generally greater interest in seeing the success of alternative fuels. He has stood on a podium with President Obama's first Chief of Staff, Rahm Emanuel, who said "I tend to disagree with most oilmen from Texas (but) I am proud to say I agree with Boone on putting more

---

* Clean Energy Fuels is also a leading member of – and key direct contributor to – NGVAmerica.

natural gas vehicles on the roads". There is some irony to this, given Pickens' long-time efforts to prevent Democrats from getting elected, perhaps best shown by his funding of groups opposing John Kerry in his bid for President in 2004 via the so-called Swift Boat controversy.

Pickens' efforts also put a spotlight on a paradox that characterizes many business people. They generally want the government to stay out of the way of business, and often bemoan government over-spending, but at the same time advocate for government spending for their pet projects. Perhaps this is the antithesis of the 'not-in-my-backyard' or NIMBY, crowd: a request for spending "just-in-my-backyard", or JIMBY.

Despite the gyrations regarding ongoing incentives, the 2009 Federal economic stimulus plan (the American Recovery and Reinvestment Act) was clearly a big plus for natural gas fuels, as it earmarked $300 million of matching federal funds for alternative fuels infrastructure development. CNG and LNG projects garnered the majority of that program's grants. Called a "once in a lifetime opportunity" for natural gas fuels, this program enabled some landmark CNG and LNG projects to get developed and clearly contributed to the developing momentum.

The efforts of NGVAmerica, other trade organizations (e.g., the America Natural Gas Alliance and the American Gas Association's "Drive Natural Gas" initiative) and Pickens have borne small additional fruit at the Federal level. For instance, the Obama administration has recently warmed to the idea of natural gas fuels. This has not taken a straight path since Obama focused a lot of the effort and money for alternative fuels early in his administration on plug-in electric car technology under the direction of Secretary of Energy Dr. Steven Chu. Before Chu resigned in 2013, he became frustrated with the slow pace of development of plug-in electric batteries and related technological solutions and decided to focus more of the

Department of Energy's research on natural gas fuels under a new program called ARPA-E.

However, much of the opportunity for Federal support rests in the hands of Congress. It is Congress that is in charge of continuing incentives like fuel, vehicle and infra-structure tax credits to help accelerate the development of natural gas fuels markets. It is difficult to envision that happening given the current gridlock in Washington. The industry is in particular asking for such support to jump start the next round of growth in natural gas fueled heavy duty truck fleets. Many in the industry have gone so far as to conclude that such support could sunset within five or so years because the industry is likely to be self-sustaining by then.

†††

The actions of state governments incentivizing the industry have remained important given the absence of ongoing federal support for natural gas fuels, and they have begun to fill the vacuum. In fact, it could be claimed that state governments have played a central role in getting us to this point. Most importantly, California agencies have forced large fleets to use low-emission fuels as part of their effort to improve local air quality. This has almost by default forced many fleets to use natural gas fuels. But, the "carrot" is more important than the "stick". Right now, over thirty states offer rebates on natural gas vehicles or other incentives to make them more attractive to consumers.

PART III: The Present

24

"In the Marketplace"
(Earth Wind and Fire)

Transactions between sellers and buyers in the natural gas fuels industry will continue to develop and evolve in two main ways. Let's look at this from the point of view of CNG or LNG customers, focusing on large fleets, since they will ultimately drive much of the demand.

Customers of CNG will either buy and own a CNG fueling station, absorbing the capital and operating and maintenance costs into their own cost structure (in which case, they're not buying CNG but rather pipeline gas that they "upgrade" to CNG), or pull up to a third-party fueling station and pay the station owner's price (retail, or some discount to retail if the customer has established a card-based method of payment that allows for this). These alternate approaches can be referred to as "make" or "buy", i.e., the customer will make his own CNG or buy the CNG from someone else.*

Consumers of LNG can either buy and own stations and also buy the LNG in bulk at a wholesale price, or they can refuel at a third party station. The term "make or buy" does not fully apply with LNG since, in either case, the consumer will have to buy the LNG in any event unless they own something like GE's LNG in a Box system.

There will always be suppliers of equipment to fulfill these business models. For CNG, the fueling station can be sold to end users who will then make the CNG for their own use, or to intermediaries (third parties) who will instead supply the finished CNG to end users pulling into those stations.

---

* The home refueling appliance discussed in Chapter 34 provides individuals and families with the option to take the "make" approach.

Fuel supply companies like Trillium, Love's and KwikTrip own the CNG and LNG stations and sell finished CNG and LNG to end customers, while companies like Waste Management, UPS and some of the oil and gas producers generally own the CNG and LNG stations themselves, figuring they'd rather internalize all the cost and pocket any difference compared with retail.* Companies that prefer to own their own equipment will buy CNG stations from companies like ANGI, GE and others, or LNG stations from companies like GP Strategies, Chart and Cryostar. Chart and GE also sell LNG production plants to owners and operators who then produce and sell the LNG. (The company names mentioned aren't an exhaustive list.)

Apache Corp. CNG station
Photo credit: Apache Corporation

Obviously, the long-term success of companies like Clean Energy, Trillium, Love's and Transfuels that sell the finished natural gas fuel to end users will be predicated on their competing against others supplying the same finished products. Perhaps more importantly, they must also compete against companies that decide they would rather internalize the costs and own the stations themselves.

Some large on-highway trucking fleets like UPS are committing as much as is justifiable to the latter approach. UPS is already anteing up for roughly two dozen LNG

* Of course, there are underlying factors that tend to dictate whether a company owns its own station, such as the amount of fuel consumed.

fueling stations they will place right at their depots. Even in this case, they will still use third party stations for LNG supply where it is impractical to justify an internally-owned station. In addition, their truck drivers will also have to use third-party on-highway stations when they're running low on fuel and can't make it back to base.

The LNG and CNG fuel suppliers are making every effort to capture and retain truck fleet customers by explaining that they provide value, like helping the customer avoid all the internal capital costs and offering potentially higher fuel supply reliability. By one count (source: Littlefair interview with Motley Fuel 4/14/14), there are nearly one hundred companies vying for the opportunity to sell natural gas fuels, which points to a vibrant competitive future.

Clean Energy, Transfuels, Trillium, Love's and others hope to build out enough stations that they will make it less attractive for an individual customer to build its own station. On the other hand, the larger the customer, the more vehicles it has to fuel and the more fuel it uses, the more likely it will be to take a self-sufficient approach.

†††

Other than the prospective liquefaction of natural gas at a customer site using something like GE's LNG in a Box, LNG production has a unique set of dynamics. LNG production plants can be viewed in much the same way as oil refineries.

Owners of LNG plants generally focus on running efficient low-cost operations to be able to sell the LNG in bulk at a competitive wholesale price to others or, like Clean Energy Fuels, are integrated from the plant all the way to the retail fueling station and therefore try to capture the whole value chain. It's much the same way with oil refiners, who may or may not own the fueling stations directly or have branded franchise stations, but in any event have to run efficient plants well-positioned geographically to serve their markets in order to remain competitive. In the past few decades, the large oil companies have tended to divest their stations and only focus on the refining and terminaling side of the business. (Thus, it was somewhat out of character when Shell announced plans to both produce LNG and sell it at the retail level.)

Making LNG well – efficiently, safely and reliably – is not child's play. Therefore, it's a bit surprising that so many companies have evaluated entering – or have already entered – the business of owning LNG plants to serve the merchant market. After all, these plants are quite similar to cryogenic plants for making liquid oxygen, nitrogen or carbon dioxide and few users of those products make them themselves, preferring instead to leave that operation to the industrial gas companies like Praxair and Air Products.

This enigmatic situation can be partly explained by the fact that the natural gas utilities have owned and operated many LNG plants for peak shaving since the 1970s and '80s. This has caused a sort of "if they can do it, I can do it" mentality among prospective LNG plant owners. It remains to be seen, however, how competitive the new producers can be: Will they select the right technology? Will they locate them for ideal competitiveness? Can they squeeze out costs without sacrificing safety?

25

"Let Me be Your Car"

(Elton John)

For the first time ever, you can choose among an extensive range of natural gas-fueled cars and pick-up trucks. The Honda Civic, which has been the mainstay CNG car for some time, is now available in more places than ever – Honda launched an east coast marketing and sales campaign several years ago. Since 2012, Chevy has supplied Savana cargo and passenger vans set up for CNG. In 2013, GM added the CNG fuel-equipped Chevy Silverado and GMC Sierra with 6-liter V8 engines. These are bi-fuel models, with both CNG and gasoline tanks that together give the trucks ranges of 650 miles between refills. A CNG version of the Chevy Impala is also being released and this has the potential to be important for individual consumers and taxi cab fleets. Ford has CNG F-250 pick-ups and Transit vans, and Chrysler introduced a CNG Dodge Ram truck.

Ford sold roughly 15,000 CNG cars in 2013, which is a drop in the overall car population bucket, but a clear signal that we have passed an inflection point and CNG vehicles have gained market traction. However, we are still not at the point where car companies are willing to devote production lines to CNG vehicles.

The OEMs are taking a more conservative approach for now, in some cases simply prepping the cars at the factory for CNG modifications and connecting the customers up with approved installers for completion of "factory-equivalent" cars and trucks that have full warrantees and company-backed service. Before we see full dedicated assembly lines, the car companies are more likely to take an approach already being used to make heavy-duty natural gas-fueled trucks: integrating CNG vehicles into the existing lines – say, every tenth car on the line would require CNG parts fittings, which the mechanics (and robots) would recognize and adjust for in that particular case.

The list of OEM-backed CNG cars and trucks is ever-changing and expanding, including Toyota and VW who are talking about testing the waters. Chrysler may be pulled deeper into the CNG vehicle market by its new owners at Fiat, who have extensive experience serving the needs of the large market in Italy for natural gas vehicles. Additionally, licensed converters operate in most states.*

The car manufacturers' recent decisions to take a more positive stand in the market can be attributed to several factors. The market has been jump-started to a large extent by the actions of fleets placing sizable orders of vehicles. This has finally encouraged fuel suppliers to build a rapidly growing network of stations usable by the public, echoing the goal of EPACT back in the 1990s. The most notable example was ATT's decision in 2008 and announcement in 2009 to buy eight thousand CNG-fueled vans (e.g., Ford 250s) and related vehicles over five years. Other companies like Verizon (five hundred CNG vans in 2010) and a number of oil and gas companies have each also placed vehicle orders in the hundreds.

Frankly, the vehicle options available aren't enough to generate widespread mainstream consumer support yet and it will take bold moves by the auto companies to expand their relationships with preferred conversion partners or, better yet, integrate NGV capabilities into their assembly lines. More fueling infrastructure will clearly help and one can only hope that someone will be successful in developing

---

* NGVAmerica and others in the industry provide well-heeled advice, such as avoiding uncertified and unlicensed conversion companies to make sure your vehicle meets minimum safety and performance standards. Also, be cautious when evaluating the purchase of a used CNG vehicle – among other things, you want to make certain the fuel storage tank is not too old or has been abused and that you're making safety a priority.

the plug-in natural gas home appliance for overnight home refueling described in Chapter 34 to convince the general public to seriously consider buying an NGV.

Meanwhile, we can estimate what the potential could be across North America by extrapolating from the robust Salt Lake, Utah area market: the estimated ten thousand natural gas vehicles there are spread among a population of around two million people. Given that the population in the U.S. and Canada is one hundred fifty times as large, that would translate into 1,500,000 natural gas light duty vehicles across North America – which is not a bad launching point, even if that represents less than one percent of the car population.

Then, once the fueling companies, auto companies and home refueling system developers get serious, it's not outrageous to expect the market to grow to multiples of this. Among all these factors, an economical home refueling system could be the key to get the market really moving, but why so? The answer, simple enough, is economics. CNG-fueled cars cost thousands of dollars more than comparable gasoline cars and most people won't make that up-front investment without anticipating a fuel savings that offsets the cost during ownership.

If gasoline in the future costs around $3.50–4.00 per gallon (as is typical of current forecasts) and CNG saves $1.50–2.00 per gallon, it would take ten years to recoup that investment for the typical ten to twelve thousand mile-per-year driver, too long to make it attractive for most thus stymieing demand. A home refueling system can probably extend those savings to $2.50 per gallon and maybe more, lowering the payback period to more palatable levels. Then, once high-mileage drivers that will see faster paybacks and the early adopters begin to make significant purchases of CNG cars and light-duty trucks, the OEMs will be able to build and sell more vehicles at prices closer to gasoline-fueled vehicles, creating more demand and a positive feedback loop that fosters even more growth.

A Few Words About Safety

LNG and CNG are fuels. Like gasoline and diesel, they have a tendency to burn – that's why they're used as fuels! So, there is some element of risk in using them that can't be avoided. In some ways, they are safer than conventional fuels and in some ways less safe, and anyone storing, handling or using them should be familiar with their properties and associated hazards.

Natural gas fuels tend to be less hazardous than petroleum-based fuels in one key respect: it is more difficult for them to ignite in air; and when ignited they also tend to be less explosive. Off-setting this, one should consider that CNG is highly compressed, so a rupture of a tank or release from a valve can have catastrophic consequences in the immediate surrounding area. Natural gas in the LNG form is a cryogen; it's extremely cold. So, contact with skin leads to immediate and severe freezing, and it embrittles and can shatter some materials that it comes in contact with.

Of course, this book cannot provide a comprehensive view of these issues. So the reader interested in exploring this subject further should seek out the wide range of materials on the subject, perhaps contacting any of the natural gas fuel suppliers for MSDS sheets and searching for other credible and relevant information.

26

"Highway Star"

(Deep Purple)

The most important and widely impactful news for natural gas vehicles is that they are finally now making significant in-roads into the heavy-duty truck fleet market. There have been important niches like trash collection trucks, but those are niches. Now, more and more diverse truck fleet customers are beginning to line up to buy these, while companies serving the industry such as the largest truck manufacturers and leasing companies are more confident than ever justifying investments to make it happen. Evidence first:

UPS has been a leading experimenter and subsequent advocate for natural gas trucks, first buying over 1,000 CNG-powered package delivery trucks and more recently committing to 1,000 LNG-fueled 'tractors' for long-distance trailer hauls between cities. The company doesn't have to crunch and re-crunch the numbers to determine whether it makes economic sense. They realize there's an up-front expenditure for the trucks and, more recently, for stations since they are building them for their own use. But, they can keep their tractors operating far longer than is necessary for an adequate payback – one and a half million miles, sometimes first deploying them in interstate routes and then shorter routes as they age. By that time they have more than made up their investment with significant savings.

Other large fleets are following the lead of UPS and a few other pioneers. But within a few years when even more fleets convert, they too will be seen as the leaders. Pepsico's FritoLay business is a good example and their spokesman went so far as to tell an industry audience that CNG is not an alternative fuel anymore, but rather their preferred fuel so that they need to justify decisions that *don't* involve it. Proctor & Gamble has also taken a significant step in that direction by announcing in 2013 that the company had agreed to convert twenty percent of it's for-hire carrier fleet, which runs the majority of its heavy-duty trucking operations, over to CNG. Ryder's truck rental business has also taken bold steps to encourage its lessees to use natural gas-fueled trucks in place of diesel, leasing both 18-wheeler trucks and smaller "box trucks". (Penske Truck Leasing more recently entered the natural gas truck rental business, likely spurred by Ryder's adoption.)

LNG-fueled truck
Photo credit: Ryder

After a slow and halting start, all of the heavy-duty truck OEMs have finally jumped into the supply of natural gas vehicles. Yet, the market has still not reached a critical mass, so each of these companies is calculating how much to integrate CNG and LNG truck manufacturing into their core operations. As a fallback, Agility Fuel Systems (see Chapter 8) is able to provide the necessary services to integrate the engine, fuel system, controls and truck chassis into a finished product.

By every indication, the trend towards increasing natural gas fueling of heavy-duty tractor-trailer (Class 8) trucks will continue. The key questions are: How fast and how far? Using the refuse and bus industries as an example, one could envision the number of new CNG- and LNG-fueled Class 8 trucks reaching tens of thousands per year within five to ten years and ultimately a majority share of the new Class 8 truck business in the U.S. (which is close to three hundred thousand per year).

27

"Get on the Bus"
(Destiny's Child)

Transit buses operating in municipalities and airports have been one of the biggest success stories for natural gas fuels and the reasons are varied. At least one out of five new transit buses being bought is designed for CNG, an estimated twelve to fifteen percent of all transit buses currently on the road use natural gas fuels (source: www.cngnow.com) and by one account it is as high as thirty five percent (source: Littlefair article).*

Many of these buses were bought in southern California because of state and local rules and regulations that forced fleets to use cleaner fuels to help clean up the poor local air quality in the area. The last laugh, as it were, was had by the bus fleet owners and operators who also saw significant savings. Municipal bus fleets all over southern California converted to CNG and LNG at a staggering rate during the early 2000s as a result of government rules.

Word has since spread to other parts of the country where lowering air emissions is not as highly valued, but cost savings are. Buying and using CNG buses has nevertheless had the side benefit of improving air quality in those areas too.

In El Paso, Texas, the city's Sun Metro transit fleet decided to shift all of its fleet over to natural gas for a very different reason. After experiencing a diesel fuel spill at its main depot in the early 1990s, the city had to absorb millions of dollars in clean-up expenses, an embarrassing and costly error they didn't want to repeat. Sun Metro has been using CNG for twenty years and has barely looked back at diesel, even as it has had to contend with some

* Propane is also a successful bus fuel.

operating headaches with both the buses and fueling station.

In sum, the California government's push created the opportunity to pilot natural gas buses and bring enough suppliers in to support its initiation; that created the opportunity for bus fleets in the rest of the country to come on board. Obviously, they are doing so in significant numbers.

28

"Someday My Ship Will Sail"
(Emmylou Harris)

S wedes travel into the Baltic Sea and to Finland literally by the boatload to buy liquor at much lower cost than in their home country. Cruise ships pick up passengers in Stockholm, rush east across the Baltic Sea, sometimes to ports in other countries, where the passengers party, buy their booze and head back home. Major cruise lines like Viking fill this steady business with ships that run back and forth, only stopping in Stockholm long enough to discharge the sated passengers and board the new ones.

In 2013, Viking launched the first-ever cruise ship powered entirely by LNG, a 715 foot, 2,800-passenger beauty. The Viking Grace is one of dozens of ferries, tugs and other boats in service in northern Europe that have been built in the past decade to run on LNG or a combination of LNG and diesel. In the rest of Europe, dozens more LNG boats and ships are being built or planned and hundreds more are expected by the end of the decade.

Several northern European countries have a ten year head-start on the U.S. and Canada. But, we're catching up fast and by some predictions will see hundreds of LNG-powered vessels in North America by 2020. Natural gas fuels, mostly LNG and not CNG*, are revolutionizing ocean travel in a vast sweep of change much like coal replaced wind power and petroleum displaced coal over the past few hundred years.

This started in Norway in the late 1990s through a fortunate combination of government incentives meant to reduce

---

* It is much easier to fill and store the large volumes needed using the denser liquid form.

emissions and increase availability of LNG on the Norwegian coastline from plants that initially were only meant to liquefy natural gas coming from the huge North Sea reservoirs for shipping to gas-poor regions of the world. Now, the use of LNG on sea is growing across the globe.

The International Maritime Organization (IMO) is a half-century-old global institution with 170 member nations that oversees the creation of international standards affecting such diverse areas as oil spill prevention, training of ship crews and general safety. Starting in 2008, the IMO established a set of rules governing limits on noxious emissions of sulfur oxides, nitrogen oxides and ultimately greenhouse gases in certain so-called Emission Control Areas (ECAs), which wrap around the coasts 200 miles out to sea and up navigable rivers in Europe and also in the U.S., Canada and the Caribbean.

These ECA limits have already begun going into effect and will ratchet down emissions gradually over the next few years. In so doing, they'll force ship owners and operators to either change over to LNG, use more costly low-emission fuel oil or use emission control devices called scrubbers when burning low quality fuels. All of these options require significant added costs but there's no getting around them. LNG will get a healthy slice of a fast-growing pie because its cost is half that of marine diesel.

Already – as of the end of 2013 – there were over forty ships on the drawing board in North America planning to be fueled with LNG, from ferries to cargo vessels and petroleum carriers. This is a huge potential market for natural gas fuels, in fact so large that new $100 million LNG production plants and hundreds of millions of dollars in infrastructure to deliver it to ports and from ports to ships are needed to launch the industry in that direction. And considering that every part of the coast – or even every port – needs its own supply infrastructure, there's an inevitable chicken-and-egg dilemma. How is this dilemma being overcome and, once it is, what will be the impact?

Shell Oil attempted to find a way to jump-start the LNG market for ships in the Gulf Coast and the lower Mississippi River. Shell wanted to be the first to build LNG production capacity in that area and, of course, they needed demand to justify their investment. That justification came in the form of a symbiotic relationship with a shipping company called Harvey Gulf and a deal in which Shell agreed to hire Harvey Gulf to haul diesel fuel out to its rigs in the Gulf so long as Harvey Gulf agreed to use ships that are fueled with LNG that Shell would supply. Harvey Gulf got Shell's business and Shell got Harvey Gulf to commit to buying its LNG (ironically to haul diesel fuel).

Already, Harvey Gulf is in the process of receiving six LNG-fueled ships and Shell planned to build an LNG plant at its Geismar, Louisiana refinery. However, Shell has since gotten cold feet: unsure that the size and adoption rate in nearby markets are sufficient to follow through on these, Shell has at least temporarily put the Geismar plant and others on hold.

Another company that is sparking the establishment of LNG at two other coastal locations is a container shipping company, TOTE Services.* TOTE hauls containers from the port in Jacksonville, Florida to Puerto Rico and from Tacoma, Washington to Anchorage, Alaska. Aware of impending emission rules, TOTE struck a deal with the U.S. EPA to allow the company to postpone having to reduce its fleet's air emissions in return for committing to convert four of its container ships to run on LNG.

Having made the commitment to the EPA for two LNG ships operating out of Florida and two in Washington State, TOTE then had to find a way to secure some 100 million gallons worth of LNG a year. This created problems, because neither location has LNG within several hundred

---

* Container ships generally move cargo around in 53 foot "ISO" containers. These containers can be transferred on or off the boat, as well as to rail cars and truck beds.

LNG-fueled ship
Photo credit: Harvey Gulf International Marine

miles. TOTE went out for competitive bids for the fuel and also the equipment to deliver it.

Fortunately, the natural gas utility in Georgia with four LNG peak shavers, AGL, was able to commit to supplying it from its plants there to Jacksonville, while AGL and its partner WesPac Midstream develop plans to build an LNG plant right in Jacksonville.* As of this writing, TOTE still has not figured out how to get LNG for its Tacoma fueling needs but has agreements in the works with the local utility, Puget Sound Energy.

†††

The opening up of Jacksonville as an LNG fueling hub in turn opens up all sorts of other opportunities because the city is a major inter-modal hub. That is, ships, heavy-duty trucks and trains all operate there, shuffling containers and goods around from one mode of transport to another.

---

* A partnership involving Clean Energy Fuels, GE and Ferus Natural Gas Fuels also planned to build an LNG plant in Jacksonville. It's unclear whether TOTE's award to AGL will affect those plans.

With TOTE as the anchor customer, we'll likely see other local ships, trucks and possibly trains all fueling with LNG there within a few years, not to mention this will also provide a pool of LNG that can be transported to other fueling points throughout northern and central Florida.

Jacksonville exemplifies an opportunity to build significant amounts of LNG infrastructure in other locations along our oceanic coastlines and inland waterways like the Great Lakes and Mississippi River corridors. Thus, ship-board use of LNG could be an important stimulus for more supplies of LNG available for other uses.

29

"Train Kept A-Rollin"
(Aerosmith)

O f all the industries in North America that could be called conservative and slow to change, the railroads would probably make most peoples' list of the top five. Such a tendency to maintain the status quo is reasonable: the railroad companies own their own tracks and the tracks effectively confine railroad operators to specific routes. The tracks provide railroad companies with incumbent business positions that create great value for them.*

Thus, it's something of a surprise to learn that the entire rail industry changed the type of locomotion it relied on completely over a short period of only thirty years, and may do so again. In 1935, the freight and passenger rail industry was entirely reliant on steam locomotives; but, by 1965 it was almost entirely reliant on diesel-electric motors because of the nearly one-half reduction in operating costs. The rail industry is now sorting out whether the roughly one-half reduction in fuel costs by switching from diesel to natural gas, mainly in the form of LNG**, can justify another leap close to that magnitude.

Since the rail companies don't have large numbers of direct competitors to contend with, some of the impetus for pursuing cost savings has to do with competition from other forms of hauling goods, mainly from ships and trucks. LNG obviously holds significant potential to save

---

* There are only two major railroads operating in the western U.S. – Union Pacific and BNSF, and two in the eastern U.S. – CSX and Norfolk Southern.
** The regional passenger rail system in Chicago-land is converting to CNG using over $50 million of public funds.

the railroads money, help them compete for market share and improve their profit margins.

How significant could this be? Just one railroad company, Union Pacific, claims to be the second largest consumer of diesel fuel in the United States after the U.S. Navy and the differential between LNG and diesel prices is large. Another top railroad, BNSF, was bought out by Warren Buffett's Berkshire Hathaway in 2010. It's obvious that this magnitude of savings can create significant shareholder value and Buffett is the type of savvy business owner who would be keen to unlock this value.

As noted in Chapter 9, the first step towards using LNG for locomotives took place several decades ago, but the economics were not compelling and the efforts were largely abandoned. Some of the equipment that was used in the 1990s has been dusted off and reused recently in new trials. The most recent efforts were kicked off north of the U.S.-Canada border by Canadian National Railway in partnership with Vancouver's Westport Innovations and Montreal's Gaz Metro, who ran trials using LNG starting in 2012–2103. Canadian National Railway decided before the end of 2013 to advance the use of LNG from trials to commercial status. These efforts were being closely watched by other rail companies, of course, and BNSF, Union Pacific and CSX all decided in 2013 to run their own trials.

So, progress in this realm is being made and arguably the snowball is rolling. But, lots of money will be needed to convert a sizable share of the rail industry to LNG. New LNG storage tanks need to be located on tracks at regular intervals and that alone will cost hundreds of millions of dollars. New LNG production facilities to serve the demand could cost billions of dollars. New LNG fuel tender cars (rail cars with tanks attached to the locomotives because not enough LNG can be carried on the locomotives themselves) and engines optimized for LNG will cost a million dollars or more for every train.

Given this, we'll probably see a slow roll-out of LNG for this purpose, starting with trains that go back and forth along dedicated routes and those that can piggyback on new supplies at ship ports, then expanding to other rail corridors until these corridors are finally connected in a spider web-like matrix of LNG-fueled systems. Will this be accomplished within 30 years, the same time-frame as the previous conversion from steam to diesel? Only time will tell.

30

"Texas Flood"

(Stevie Ray Vaughan)

I n 2009, Clean Energy Fuels practically owned the Texas market for LNG fuel, as well as CNG stations (and hence the amount of CNG dispensed). That status had been earned by the company's purchase of the only LNG plant from Ken Kelley's original company, Applied LNG Technologies, and CNG stations built over the years to serve the major metropolitan areas. But business, like nature, abhors a vacuum so in the intervening years as the natural gas fuels growth inflection point has been reached, the landscape has dramatically changed. The anticipated demand growth has spawned new entrants consisting of a mélange of petroleum companies expanding into natural gas fuels, LNG companies from other areas flexing their muscles in Texas and entirely new start-up companies.

Ken Kelley's legacy resurfaced again with another company now vying for dominance in Texas. As noted before, Kelley sold his stake in the plant that was supposed to be placed in Peru to his ex-partner George Yates. Yates, in turn, became aware of the growing opportunity for LNG in the United States and particularly in Texas where the drilling and hydraulic fracturing markets were growing, and decided to erect the plant there via HEYCO Energy Group. HEYCO is proceeding with its plans to build a plant half way between Houston and the booming Eagle Ford Shale oil and gas basin in south Texas.

Meanwhile, the current owners of Applied LNG Technologies (including bond investors PIMCO) are also planning to build a plant west of Dallas using a design similar to Topock's. Another company, Stabilis Energy, started up by oil men Casey and Will Crenshaw (just like HEYCO and Clean Energy Fuels were started by oil men) also announced plans in 2013 for a new plant half way between San Antonio and Corpus Christi, deep in the heart of the Eagle Ford shale. Stabilis expects to also build another plant in western Texas.

To lower their costs and potentially speed up permitting, Stabilis has announced a deal with the privately-owned Koch Industries' subsidiary Flint Hills Resources to co-locate the LNG plants at Flint Hills' refineries. Stabilis also has affiliates that build LNG application equipment and supply services to the oil and gas companies. Stabilis looks like a contender, especially since it is poised to become a player in the whole LNG value chain. It is already considering building another plant in West Texas and acquired Encana's natural gas fueling assets in 2014 after the latter decided to exit the business.

Others are also considering building new LNG plants, including a company named Lynx Operating that is planning to construct a plant in west Texas. Yet another start-up called LNG America plans to haul LNG out of one of the first export terminals being built in the U.S., directly over the border from Texas in Sabine Pass, Louisiana. All told, and even excluding these last two sources, Texas is within sight of having enough LNG to fuel five thousand tractor trailers, or five hundred drilling rigs or thirty to forty hydraulic fracturing systems. On the flip side, it's easy to envision a scenario where that amount of demand will emerge in Texas in the next five-ten years. Some of this demand will develop as a result of the push for more natural gas fueling of trucks, including support by the state government for The Texas Triangle. This is a natural gas fueling corridor spanning the highways between Houston, San Antonio, Austin and Dallas that was patterned after the Interstate Clean Transportation Corridor designed for the western U.S. in the 1990s.

The Texas Triangle will also benefit CNG-fueled trucks, quite possibly on a scale even larger than LNG trucks. One company to recognize this and jump ahead of the curve is Love's, the owner of over three hundred truck stops across the U.S. After opening its first CNG fueling facilities for heavy-duty trucks in Oklahoma in 2012, the company already had plans to open eight public CNG stations in the Texas Triangle by the end of 2013. In fact, that quickly put Love's nearly on par with the number of Clean Energy Fuels' CNG stations in Texas, and Love's locations are, by some accounts, better located to serve the majority of tractor trailers plying the Texas highways.

It's safe to say that the state of Texas, which is nearly synonymous with the petroleum industry, is now poised to take a leading role in the switch to natural gas fuels.

31

"Blame Canada"
(South Park)

T his book has focused predominantly on the progress of natural gas fuels in the U.S. However, it wouldn't be complete without providing a brief view of the situation in Canada, both because so many of the advancements can be attributed to companies there, but also because it provides a unique case study by which those in the U.S. can learn.

Canada has just a bit more than one-tenth the population and Gross Domestic Product of the U.S., but on a basis proportional to those figures it puts the efforts of U.S. companies in the natural gas fuels industry to shame. For instance, the Vancouver, B.C.-based Westport Innovations and its Cummins Westport JV have almost single-handedly sustained the availability of natural gas-fueled engines through the highs and lows over the past twenty years or so. Just as importantly, the spark of enormous change in the industry arising from the use of natural gas fuels in oil and gas drilling operations owes itself to a Canadian company, Encana.

There are other examples, including the leadership in the commercial use of LNG in locomotives over the past few years by Canadian National Railway, working with Westport and the Montreal-based utility and LNG producer Gaz Metro. In sum, then, we can point to the activities of Canadian firms as being instrumental in every one of the major natural gas fuels market sectors except perhaps for marine.

There is a striking parallel between the actions and impacts of the governments in Canada and U.S., since the federal governments in both countries have been reluctant to support the natural gas fuels industry, while the far-western province of British Columbia has provided significant financial support for technology and market development much like the government in the far-western state of California largely led the United States in, and into, the use of LNG and CNG for many years.

PART IV: The Future

32

"Crossroads"
(Robert Johnson)

Recapping the status of natural gas fuels for a moment, recall that the numbers of NGVs in many countries far exceeds that of the U.S.'s car-based economy. Obviously, the adoption of NGVs at significant levels in our domestic passenger car population (where some seven million vehicles are sold annually) and in heavy-duty trucks (where nearly three hundred thousand are sold annually) would mean a dramatic shift in our fueling habits. Consider that natural gas-fueled buses and refuse collection trucks account for a large share of all such vehicles sold in the U.S. and it is possible to see that such a shift is clearly possible.

We've already seen that Clean Energy Fuels and Transfuels each plan to build LNG fueling stations along major fueling corridors. Similarly, Trillium announced in June 2013 that it plans to open at least one hundred new CNG stations in 29 states and Love's also plans to build out infrastructure. Between such retailers and companies like UPS and oil & gas companies that are building stations to serve themselves, we'll likely see a thousand new natural gas fueling stations serving tens of thousands of big trucks and light-duty vehicles within a few years.

As in any dynamic business area, the companies in the business are changing as some divest and others invest through acquisitions. We've seen that the aging owners of the private company Brown & Wagner decided by 2011 to sell Trillium and Pinnacle holdings, while the utilities were just re-ramping their efforts in natural gas fuels, so Integrys snapped up these firms. More recently, the corporate catalyst for accelerated growth, Encana, decided

Natural gas refueling station
Photo credit: Apache Corporation

it had to reserve its capital, so sold its holdings in natural gas fueling to the recent promising upstart, Stabilis.

Of course, we can expect many more such moves in the coming years – some companies will not be able to deal with the roller coaster ride inevitably posed by such a vibrant new business area, while some will seize the perceived opportunity and enter the market or grow their positions further from the disposition of assets by others.

†††

There are two specific areas we'll focus on as we wrap up this book: One is the opportunity to make the natural gas industry truly "green" by using methane from landfills and food and other wastes. The other is the possibility of widespread home refueling of natural gas cars and trucks, which would truly be a game changer for the personal vehicle market.

33

"We Are Happy Landfill"
(Gorillaz)

The controversy over hydraulic fracturing that is swirling around the production techniques used to extract most of our natural gas now is in part driven by environmentalists' interest in seeing the U.S. and rest of the world transition rapidly to renewable fuels like biodiesel and to renewable energy sources like solar and wind. There is some irony here, since many of the same people that advocated the use of natural gas over coal as recently as five years ago now widely oppose natural gas. Obviously, they are drawing a new line in the sand.

Another widespread source of methane exists, however. With appropriate government prompting and support, combined with market demand, this "renewable" source or methane could have a significant impact on the future nature of natural gas fuels.

Renewable natural gas fuels used in trucks, for instance, reduce greenhouse gas emissions by 80–90 percent compared with diesel. That compares with a far smaller, but still nice-to-have, 20–30 percent reduction in greenhouse gas emissions from conventional natural gas sources. Accordingly, they'd be much easier for environmentalists to get on-board with.*

There are three pathways that can be used to produce renewable natural gas fuels and each provides some opportunities for the industry and customers looking for a greener approach.

---

* The reader interested in this area would do well to visit the website of Energy Vision, an advocacy organization at the forefront of promoting renewable natural gas fuels: www.energy-vision.org.

Focusing on one approach, the renewable LNG plant at Waste Management's Altamont, California landfill proves that production of renewable natural gas fuels at significant scale in one centralized location is possible. This plant can fuel up to roughly three hundred trucks. Most landfills are too small to support this scale of LNG production, but it would be feasible for factory farm food producers like Cargill and ADM.

These food production companies create a lot of waste material as a byproduct of their processing operations. These wastes can quite easily be cooked in a process called bio-digestion to make methane and then liquefied to LNG at those sites for distribution to multiple fueling stations. We may well see plants like this in the future.*

In the second approach, enough renewable CNG can be produced at small landfills and farms to fuel up to a few dozens of trucks or cars. A large dairy operation, Fair Oaks Farms, runs milk trucks to processors using renewable CNG produced from its bio-digested manure piles and the company BioCNG specializes in building this sort of fuel production and dispensing scheme at tiny scales.

The third approach is the most promising. It is exemplified by Clean Energy Fuel's investment in the McCommas landfill outside Dallas and a dozen or so other similar projects to date. This approach involves cleaning up the biogas, like at the Altamont plant. But instead of liquefying it on-site, the methane is put into a pipeline that can transport it somewhere else where it can be liquefied at an LNG plant or "captured" at many CNG stations even hundreds or thousands of miles away.

There's a bit of accounting sleight of hand involved with this approach: Once you put natural gas into a pipeline at point "A", it comingles with all the other natural gas so you can't trace those molecules to point "B". The industry,

---

* It's difficult to store enough CNG at a landfill or food waste facility to make this approach viable on a large scale.

supported by regulators, acknowledges that those renewable methane molecules wind up somewhere, so businesses can take credit for them wherever they make the CNG or LNG. Thus, Clean Energy Fuels "wheels" the renewable molecules to its CNG stations and LNG plants, where it can be sold.*

Clean Energy began marketing this product in 2013 under the trade-name "Redeem". The company's objective is to get customers to buy a twenty percent blend; that is one part renewable CNG or LNG for every four parts conventional CNG or LNG. In that way, the product is a lot like biodiesel, which is after all only five-twenty percent actual "bio" diesel and eighty-ninety five percent regular diesel.

The Federal government incentivizes this type of renewable natural gas product under the Renewable Fuels Standards (a.k.a. RFS), which was set up as part of our domestic energy policy to help move the nation off of gasoline and diesel. The RFS established credits that renewable natural gas sellers generate and sell to petroleum companies who must each own a certain amount. Often times, the credit sells for more than what the fuel itself is worth. However, there's a rub – the value of these credits is established on an open market and the value looking out into the future is not assured. So, it's difficult for companies to bank on the uncertain value of credits when deciding to make multi-million dollar investments in renewable natural gas projects.

Estimates have been made that renewable natural gas fuels could replace over 10 billion gallons of gasoline in the U.S. per year, a sizable portion of the market. Of course, it's not realistic to expect that the actual number will be close to such levels, but this is the stuff environmentalists dream of.

---

* Wheeling is a term first coined by the electric power industry to describe moving electrons refueling technology on power lines from one area to another.

34

"Bring It on Home"
(Led Zeppelin)

As of this writing, the U.S. is adding CNG stations at a pace not seen since the early 1990s. This time, not just natural gas utilities but also private enterprises are building these stations in cities, along highways at truck stops, and at distribution and manufacturing centers. All well and good, and these efforts will continue, especially since, for the first time, so many of the OEM companies now sell CNG vehicles.

To truly blossom as a fuel for average drivers, more CNG stations are needed in more neighborhoods, making it convenient for more customers to refuel.

The missing link to even greater, and perhaps even explosive, growth in the car and light-duty truck market is a successful, low-cost, easy to install and reliable home refueling system. A system like this called "PHILL" was developed with assistance from Honda but never caught on because of high initial costs and maintenance problems. However, other companies like GE have jumped in the game to build such a device.*

At this point, GE is working with Eaton Corporation on such a unit and is targeting a price of $500 with a refueling time under an hour. Others are working on similar concepts, including BRC Fuelmaker who currently offers the PHILL system, as well as Whirlpool, the Gas Technology Institute and numerous others.

---

* If any company can squeeze costs out of a home refueling system, make it reliable and market it widely, that company just might be GE. They could even market a home refueling system along with stoves, clothes dryers and other natural gas appliances.

Once home refueling technology has become successful, it's easy to imagine consumers buying CNG refueling "appliances" at local stores and having them hooked up by qualified technicians (perhaps contractors from local gas utilities). Hundreds of thousands or millions of these units could go into operation in garages wherever there is local natural gas service (which is over one half of the homes in the U.S., roughly sixty million) across the U.S. This is analogous to plug-in electric vehicles that also refuel during down times, usually at night. In the case of home natural gas refueling systems, you could fuel at a cost far below that of gasoline and then jump in your car and easily travel 300–400 miles.

Plug-in electric vehicles have begun to succeed, with the Chevy Volt, Tesla and other cars serving a growing, excited and promising market. Once home CNG refueling appliances become widely available, it's easy to envision that plug-in natural gas systems (maybe trademarked "PING!" to create some branding buzz) and hence vehicles, could become far more popular.

35

"Heroes"
(David Bowie)

T he Preface pointed out a major premise of this book: That significant change in the world tends to be brought about by highly motivated individuals, often working against the norms and status quo of society and existing businesses. These people can be labeled the contrarians, pioneers, believers and Kool-Aid® drinkers.

I've pointed out some of these: Ken Kelley working on a cleaner fuel motivated by his father's possible death-by-diesel to get LNG fuel and equipment deployed and supplied to fleets in the west; T. Boone Pickens working his own billionaire-based magic to start and finance Clean Energy Fuels and singlehandedly lobby the government for support; and others like Merritt Norton, George Yates and Casey Crenshaw who have come more recently into the fray, but potentially with no less significant future impact. There are other people who I have made little, if any, mention of directly or by their affiliations (GTI's Bill Liss and Ryder Truck's Scott Perry to name a few), as well as start-ups that we'll have to take a wait and see attitude with (e.g., REV LNG, which was started by Preston Hoopes, a Pennsylvania turf farmer).

Consultants often get a bad rap as talkers not doers, but in this case people like Cliff Gladstein and Eric Neandross (Gladstein Neandross & Associates), Pat LaStrapes and Bob Nimocks (Zeus Intelligence) and Jon Lear (Ruby Mountain) have greatly influenced and in some cases actually led the development of concepts and efforts.

Most of these individuals have been involved in the natural gas fuels industry for at least a decade, some much longer, and most also show no signs of slowing down.

As the natural gas fuels industry matures, both market and technology developments will likely be increasingly driven by large companies like GE and Shell, and the major car, truck and engine suppliers. But, for the time being the promise of natural gas is still largely the domain of small companies and the individuals within them who are willing to take risks, wield their influence and drive change forward.

AFTERWORD For Investors

Companies involved in alternative fuels like natural gas tend to attract investors. After all, who wouldn't want to participate in an industry that can help reduce our reliance on foreign oil (therefore improve our national security) and improve local air quality and reduce greenhouse gas emissions, all the while reducing costs for consumers running cars, operators of large truck fleets and others? People who are drawn to invest for such reasons are emotional investors. The energy independence and environmental angles tend to draw in these emotional investors, while educated investors are drawn to the value that can be created when a company provides economic benefits.

Emotional investors drive a lot of the passion in these stocks, placing bets, commenting on public message boards and creating word-of-mouth excitement with their friends and family. But they tend to be only a small share of total investors. Emotional investors have a tendency to take a buy-and-hold strategy and often stick with their investments too long. They're constantly convinced the subject company is on the brink of a breakthrough in sales growth, profitability, or perhaps technology, even when the evidence suggests otherwise.

This type of investor is a true believer and feels the company's mission is noble and deserves support. It's common in environmental and alternative energy and fuel businesses—there are many, many examples. One of the most notorious was a company called Molten Metal Technologies that operated in the 1990s, taking a technology invented by U.S. Steel for destroying waste and driving the stock's market value to $900 million before imploding and being sold for less than $1 million. The emotional investors were dazzled by the concept of the technology, which helped push up demand for the stock. But many investors lost money in the stock value's downward spiral. Those who were burned included institutional investors, some of whom shied away from environmental technologies for years to come as a result of the experience.

The same potential danger exists in the natural gas fuels space and we can examine the course of stock values for four companies in the business to exemplify some key points.

To take the first example, Clean Energy Fuels (CLNE) has extremely vocal advocates that populate the public message boards and defend the stock at all cost, as well as detractors who bash it constantly. All opinions have some validity, but the real issue is: How has the stock actually performed and what is its outlook?

Clean Energy Fuels went public in 2007 at $12.00 per share and it's bounced around since, but has not shown any kind of consistent upward trend. In, fact, the stock hit a high of about $23.00 per share in March 2012 but declined by almost two-thirds from that level by early 2014. Of course, Clean Energy Fuels may break out to the upside, but emotional buy-and-hold investors have done much more poorly than, say, long-term investors in S&P, Dow Jones or NASDAQ indexes, or traders who have well-timed their trades during the price fluctuations.*

Chart Industries (GTLS) is our second example. As noted in the profile (Chapter 20), Chart had been a prime force in supplying equipment to the LNG fueling industry in the 1990s and early 2000s before folding up that tent when the industry stalled and then re-entering it in the late 2000s. The stock price scraped at between $5 and $10 per

---

* It's worth pondering that buy-and-hold investors in a value stock like Citibank have done about as well over the past five year stretch as they have in Clean Energy Fuels, nominally a growth stock.

share at the bottom of the Great Recession in 2009, before recovering to around $20 per share from mid 2009 to late 2010. Then, the LNG business opportunity helped cause the stock price to rocket up to a high of over $120 per share in late 2013. It has since settled below $100.

Any well-informed investor timing his or her investment in Chart when early indications were the LNG market would take off would have done well. On the other hand, an investor that jumped on board the stock at the height of the 2013 frenzy would just as readily have lost over one-third of his or her money in as little as four months.

Westport Innovations (profiled in Chapter 21) was formed in 1995 and went public in 1999 on the Toronto Stock Exchange. The stock price of Westport Innovations has had an even more volatile history than Chart. Early in its history while it was developing and announcing critical partnerships, there was a significant amount of investor interest as well as a high emotional investment quotient. In its first full year as a public company, fiscal year 2000, the stock price rose more than ten-fold, from less than $2.00 to over $26.00 per share. Optimism and pessimism have battled for the upper hand while the company has continued to tweak its business approach and technology mix, all the while still staying at least partially true to its "HPDI" technology roots.

Since the most recent deep share price bottom, Westport's stock rose by more than ten-fold (again), from about $3.00 in 2009 to over $48.00 in early 2012. From there, it dropped two-thirds over the next two years (just like Clean Energy Fuels' stock price did), as the company experienced a string of problems, including delays in the release of the all-important Cummins Westport 12-liter engine, the decision to postpone further work on the 15-liter HPDI engine for heavy-duty trucks and the recall of twenty five thousand vehicles that use Cummins Westport engines. Just as with the other companies riding the start-up roller coaster, investment timing has been critical to success.

Another example of a company that is deeply involved in the natural gas fuels business, but has also taken stakes in other alternative energy areas, is provided by Quantum Fuel Systems Technologies (QTWW), which was started up in 2000 and then spun out of another company, IMPCO, in 2002. At that time, Quantum was focused on hydrogen fuel and fuel cell technology, along with natural gas fuels – mainly systems for CNG – and a few other odds and ends.

Over the course of its first few years in business, Quantum focused increasingly on hydrogen fueling because hydrogen fuels had the policy and financial support of the Bush administration. Over the span of a decade after going public, natural gas fuels became less and less important for Quantum, to the point where it was barely mentioned in 10-K's and other public filings. When it was mentioned, it was typically in the context of foreign markets like China and India. As the hydrogen fuel market then struggled, Quantum's stock dropped to $2 per share from a split-adjusted value of $800, a decline of more than ninety nine percent. Obviously, the buy-and-hold true believers were badly hurt.

Then, signaling that the natural gas fuels marketplace has become a hot area for investors and with strong technology in CNG storage tanks and a growing backlog of business, Quantum's stock rose from $2 to $10 in just the six months between September 2013 and March 2014. Savvy, emotionally-detached investors were able to follow the fundamentals of the industry and Quantum's technical capabilities and placed educated winning bets on the prospects for the company. In sum, it is only recently that Quantum has focused so intently on natural gas fueling to the exclusion of other business areas and has since ridden a 500% increase in its share value as a result of strong technology positioning.

†††

Of course, this book does not provide specific investment advice, but we can summarize tips that may be drawn from these examples. They pertain both to natural gas fuels businesses and many other alternative energy industries (not to mention all start-ups, which are inherently risky), and can be borne in mind by both retail and institutional investors, as well as any company looking into making a strategic investment or acquisition:

- Be prepared for extreme volatility.
- Take the long view, but be willing to trade on a short-term basis. Natural gas fuels should have a long-term upward trajectory but during any short-term period there will be varying market dynamics creating positive or negative fundamental trends. This will affect each company differently and, moreover, every company's actions will create its own stock price trends.
- Timing is everything. Investors that made the right timing calls made very high returns on their money in every one of these stocks. Others that made moves at the wrong time took a bath.
- Be prepared to study the ebb and flow of the overall industry, as well as the specific segment involved, e.g., CNG versus LNG and equipment suppliers versus owners-operators of equipment that supply the fuels.
- Look for industry turning points, whether positive or negative, and be prepared to buy and sell accordingly. If you want to be a long-term supporter, consider selling when it appears that is the prudent thing to do and be prepared to buy back in at the appropriate time.
- Separate emotional attachments in a stock from educated investment considerations. Go ahead and invest in a company because you believe in their mission. If you want to support something because you like it, fine. But consider your investment like a vacation in Las Vegas: Don't count on coming home with your money.

- The natural gas fuels industry is exciting, promising and potentially a good area to invest in. But, don't expect any specific company involved to mimic, say, Microsoft's market dominance and stock performance during their glory days of 1986–2000.

†††

Meanwhile, private equity and venture capital companies and strategic investors have begun to pick through private natural gas fuel companies looking for investment plays. For example, the bond investment behemoth, PIMCO, a company that manages $2 trillion in assets, invested several years ago in Applied LNG Technologies (Ken Kelley's firm originally). Since then, ALT has moved forward with plans to double the size of its Topock, Arizona LNG plant and build a plant on a greenfield site in Texas. Taking a somewhat different approach, in 2013 GE made a strategic investment by acquiring the private LNG plant builder, Salof, outright.

How else can we spot this increased appetite for corporate investment in natural gas fuels? To take but one example, there has been significant growth in the number of employees from I-banks and venture capital firms walking the natural gas fuel tradeshow floors in the past few years.

INDEX